THE DISCOVERY
OF THE ANCIENT WORLD

THE DISCOVERY
OF THE ANCIENT WORLD

BY

HARRY E. BURTON

Select Bibliographies Reprint Series

 BOOKS FOR LIBRARIES PRESS
FREEPORT, NEW YORK

First Published 1932
Reprinted 1969

STANDARD BOOK NUMBER:
8369-5113-1

LIBRARY OF CONGRESS CATALOG CARD NUMBER:
75-102228

PRINTED IN THE UNITED STATES OF AMERICA

PREFACE

THOUGH much has been written on the subject, the history of ancient geography has received from students of classical literature and the history of Greece and Rome less attention than it deserves. It has seemed to me, therefore, that a brief treatment of the subject, giving the most essential facts, arranged, so far as possible, in chronological order, might be useful. At the risk of detracting from the interest of the book I have endeavored always to be concise, omitting stories of ancient writers which might have been entertaining and theories of modern writers which might have been stimulating. In general I have studiously avoided the discussion of disputed points, adopting the principle of Livy: "haec et his similia, utcumque animadversa aut existimata erunt, haud in magno equidem ponam discrimine." Those who are interested will find ample material for study in the bibliography at the end of the book.

I am indebted to many books, but especially to the very complete and scholarly treatment of the subject by E. H. Bunbury in his *History of Ancient Geography*.

H. E. B.

HANOVER, NEW HAMPSHIRE
   May, 1932

CONTENTS

LIST OF MAPS

THE DISCOVERY
OF THE ANCIENT WORLD

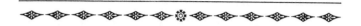

THE DISCOVERY
OF THE ANCIENT WORLD

I. *Introduction*

I⊤ is a fact constantly reiterated that we are indebted to the Greeks for the development of literature, art, and architecture. It is also well known
that the foundations of modern government and law
were laid by the Romans. But it is not often said, if,
indeed, it is generally appreciated, that we are indebted to the Greeks and Romans for the discovery
of a large part of the world. This discovery, covering
a period of more than a thousand years, the gradual
acquisition of knowledge of lands and waters more
and more remote, is a story full of interest to the general reader and of very practical and definite value to
the student of ancient history or literature. In comparatively recent times we have been thrilled by the
exploration of central Africa, by efforts to reach the
poles. Among the Greeks and Romans this venturing
into the unknown was a common experience, undertaken again and again for the purpose of trade, colonization, or conquest, with inadequate equipment and
supplies. The expedition of Alexander, in courage, in
faith, and in its contribution to the knowledge of the

world, is comparable only with the first voyage of Columbus.

It is even popularly supposed that the ancients thought that the earth was flat. On the contrary, in the third century before Christ Eratosthenes said that, if the Atlantic Ocean were not so large, one could sail around the earth, and Strabo,[1] two centuries later, suggested the possibility of another continent between western Europe and eastern Asia, thus anticipating by 1500 years the discovery of America. As early as the sixth century before Christ Pythagoras had taught the spherical shape of the earth, and in this he was followed by Aristotle in the fourth century. It is probable that from this time educated persons in general believed that the earth was round, though there were still some, like Tacitus, who were unconvinced.

In matters of geographical detail there are many blunders in the Greek and Latin writers, due to various causes. The subject was not formally taught in the schools and there were no textbooks or maps adapted to use in the class-room. But many mistakes in location or direction are the result, not of individual ignorance, but of prevailing misconceptions due to the lack of scientific instruments for determining latitude and longitude. The first chapter of Caesar's *Gallic War* will serve as an example, in spite of the doubt that exists regarding the authenticity of the passage. There it is stated that Aquitania faces northwest, Gaul (in the restricted sense) north, and

[1] i, 4, 6.

Belgium northeast, whereas it would properly be said that Aquitania faces west, Gaul west or northwest, and Belgium north. The mistake arises from a general misconception of the direction of the western coast of Gaul, an error that appears constantly in the writings of the geographers.

With very rare exceptions the Greeks and Romans were not scientific geographers, nor were the constant additions to their knowledge of the earth's surface properly recorded and published. There were very few explorations for the express purpose of acquiring geographical information. The ancient world was discovered through the medium of traders or colonists, and as a by-product of military or naval expeditions. Thus, Alexander opened up the East and Caesar added Gaul to the western world. But military and naval commanders were interested primarily in the success or failure of their expeditions, not in contributions to knowledge. Traders were generally uneducated men with an eye to business only, and their voyages and observations were rarely recorded. Under these circumstances it is not surprising that the development of geographical knowledge was slow and that we find many blunders in the Greek and Latin writers. Interest in geography began in Greece about 500 years before Christ and, after that, many books were published, most of them quite unscientific and many of them existing now only in fragments. In the Roman period far more of the earth's surface was known, but sources of information were little more reliable and the treatment was no more scholarly.

Beyond acquainting themselves with the location of places most often mentioned in classical authors, modern readers, even classical scholars, have in general paid little attention to geography, and, beyond noting the blunders in Greek and Latin literature, they have rarely any adequate conception of the geographical knowledge of the Greeks and Romans. The works of many of the ancient geographers are lost and, even if they survived, would probably be little read. How many classical scholars are familiar with the works of Strabo and Pomponius Mela, descriptive treatments that are full of interest and valuable information, even if they are not highly regarded as literature? How many students of Caesar know that it was the prevailing notion that the Seine, the Loire, and the Garonne all flowed into the English Channel? How many students of Horace know just what the author has in mind when he speaks of the Scythians? The teacher of Greek and Latin would often find it tremendously helpful to know the state of geographical knowledge in the lifetime of the author he may be reading.

II. *Discovery of the Mediterranean Sea*

WHEN we speak of the discovery of a part of the world we mean that a region, hitherto known only to its own inhabitants, has been visited and more or less explored by other people, usually of a more powerful or more highly civilized race. Now, since the discovery of the world was initiated and carried on by peoples living upon the shores of the Mediterranean

Sea, it is necessary to consider which of those peoples first visited parts of that sea remote from their own lands, that is, who may be said to have discovered the Mediterranean Sea as a whole. In this connection we must consider the Egyptians, the Cretans, and the Phoenicians, who successively, in one way or another, were important peoples in the Mediterranean world before the development of Greek civilization.

Regarding the Egyptians there is little to be said. They were not an active commercial race, did not send out colonies, and, though they sent expeditions into Persia as early as the sixteenth century before Christ, were during most of their history not ambitious for foreign conquest. It is doubtful if their definite geographical knowledge in the pre-Greek period extended far beyond the Nile valley, Crete, the eastern coast of the Mediterranean, and the Red Sea. Vague information about more distant places must have come to them from traders who supplied their needs — those who traveled by sea from Crete or Phoenicia, or by caravan from more remote parts of Asia. According to Herodotus, in the reign of King Necho a Phoenician expedition circumnavigated Africa, and, if the story is true, the Egyptians of the time must have had some knowledge of the continent on which they lived. In the matter of geographical discovery, however, the Egyptians themselves may be regarded as almost negligible.

The Cretans, on the other hand, were a commercial people and were probably the first to become familiar with a large part of the Mediterranean basin. They were the real discoverers. There is evidence of their influence, if not of their actual presence, not only on the islands of the Aegean Sea and the coast of Greece, but in many places in southern Italy and Sicily and probably even in Sardinia and Spain. There was a legend that the temple at Eryx was built by Daedalus; another, that Minos, on an expedition, was killed in Sicily, and his tomb was actually shown at Agrigentum. It is obvious that in the period of the so-called Minoan or Aegean civilization (roughly speaking, 3000 to 1200 years before Christ) there was intercourse from one end of the Mediterranean to the other.

The comparatively recent discovery of evidences of Cretan activity in various parts of the Mediterranean world has reduced the importance of the Phoenicians, who were formerly regarded as the only precursors of the Greeks in the trade and colonization of the Mediterranean. Now, though there was undoubtedly overlapping, we must assume that the Phoenicians were the successors of the Cretans in the trade and settlement of the Mediterranean coasts, occupying the interval between the decline of the Aegean civilization and the development of the civilization of historical Greece, and probably extending definite geographical knowledge further to the west than their predecessors. They were the chief navigators of the Mediterranean at the time when the Homeric poems were written. Unlike the Cretans they left little archaeological evidence. Our knowledge of the early commercial and colonizing activity of the Phoenicians is based upon traditions preserved in the Greek writers and upon names and religious cults that survived in historical Greece. They settled on many of the islands of the Aegean Sea, on the shores of Thrace, and, further west, in Sicily, northern Africa, and southern Spain, long before the coming of the Greek colonies. Though they apparently had no literature, the Greeks were indebted to them for their alphabet, which is found in its oldest form on the islands of Thera and Melos, where there were Phoenician settlements. Gades, in southern Spain, is said to have been founded by the Phoenicians 1100 years before Christ, and the name Tartessus, which is Tarshish in Phoenician and the Scriptures, is applied by Greek and Roman writers either generally to southern Spain, to the river Baetis, or to a city. The ancient name of the Strait of Gibraltar, the Pillars of Hercules, is of Phoenician origin, Hercules being the Phoenician god Melkart. On the northern coast of Africa, Utica was a Phoenician settlement, and Carthage, founded much later, ultimately became the most powerful of all the Phoenician colonies.

It has been thought that the Phoenicians sailed up the western coast of Europe to the Tin Islands, the Cassiterides, from which came the tin used in the manufacture of bronze. This is possible, but hardly probable. Cornwall, in southwestern Britain, was undoubtedly the source of the tin supply, and was ignorantly regarded as another island in the group of the Scilly Islands. It is difficult to believe that the Phoenicians sailed as far as this. Indeed, it is unlikely that they went farther north than the mouth of the river Baetis in Spain. The tin was in all probability brought by local traders to Tartessus or Gades, and from there was carried by the Phoenicians to the eastern Mediterranean.

Those who have credited the Phoenicians with voyages to the Tin Islands have found little difficulty in carrying them still farther, even into the Baltic Sea, in search of amber for the Mediterranean trade. The northern coast of Germany was the chief source of amber, which in very early times may have traveled by sea from Jutland to southern Spain; later, it was carried up the rivers of Germany and then overland to the head of the Adriatic Sea. Interesting evidence of this is found in the name of the river Eridanus, which in the ancient writers was constantly associated with the amber trade. It was originally regarded as a river in the extreme north, flowing into the northern ocean.[1] Later, however, the Greeks gave the name to the river Po, and here they localized the story of Phaethon and his sisters, who shed tears of amber. But there was no amber in this region. Evidently it was simply the place of distribution. There is after all no indication that the Phoenicians had anything to do with the amber trade, and, in fact, there is no tradition of their settlement on either side of the Adriatic. It is probable, however, that they did not neglect opportunities for trade at the head of that sea.

From what has been said it is obvious that the Cretans, and, probably to a much greater extent, the

[1] Herod., iii, 115.

Phoenicians, were familiar with the lands of the Mediterranean basin. There is no evidence, however, that their knowledge extended far inland, though some information must have been brought to them by traders from the interior. The geographical knowledge of these peoples was not recorded, so far as we know, and in the Homeric poems we find little definite geographical information outside of Greece, the Aegean Sea, and the coast of Asia Minor. And yet it is very difficult to assume that the geographical knowledge of the Phoenicians was not passed on to the Greeks.

III. *The Voyage of the Argonauts*

THAT the story of the Argonauts was known to the author of the *Odyssey* is apparent from the following passage (xii, 69-72), the only reference to it in the Homeric poems: "Returning from Aeetes, the Argo, known to all, escaped the Clashing Rocks, by the aid of Hera." If we had an account of this mythical voyage in its original form, it would perhaps throw some light upon the geography of the pre-Homeric and Homeric periods. As it is, the versions that we have simply illustrate the geographical knowledge or ignorance of successive writers who give the story in more or less detail.

It may be noted that the voyage is not, as might be expected, confined to the Aegean Sea and the Black Sea. It was a comparatively easy task for the travelers to reach Colchis on the river Phasis, which flowed into the eastern end of the Black Sea.[1] But, as in the case of Odysseus and Menelaus returning from Troy, it was a very difficult matter to reach home again, and in the various writers we find the *Argo* making a wide circuit, either to the north or to the south. Thus, the "Clashing Rocks" in the passage from the *Odyssey* already quoted appear to be in the western Mediterranean near Scylla and Charybdis, though most of the other writers identify them with the Symplegades or Cyaneae, two small islands at the northern end of the Bosphorus.

Except the brief allusion in the *Odyssey*, the first account of the voyage is in a quotation from Hesiod given by the scholiast on Apollonius Rhodius, iv, 259 and 284. According to this, the Argonauts sailed along the river Phasis into the eastern ocean and then around to the southern coast of Africa, whence they carried the *Argo* overland to the Mediterranean. Since the Phasis is a small river, this is interesting evidence of the idea of the time that the eastern ocean was only a short distance east of the Black Sea. The same conception appears in a fragment of Mimnermus (about 600 B.C.), to the effect that the city of Aeetes, King of Colchis, lies on the edge of the eastern ocean. The first full account of the voyage is found in Pindar, *Pythian*, iv. He describes the return much as Hesiod had given it. The idea that the boat was carried overland from the southern coast of Africa to the Mediterranean is not quite so surprising if we

[1] For a very different interpretation of the original story see W. Dörpfeld, *Homers Odyssee*, pp. 262 ff.

realize that the Greeks of the time knew nothing of the great southern extension of the African continent.

Quite different routes are given by the geographer Scymnus (quoted by the scholiast on Apollonius Rhodius, iv, 284) and by Apollonius himself. According to the former, the *Argo* sailed from the Black Sea up the river Tanais to the northern ocean and then west and south to the Pillars of Hercules. Apollonius gives free rein to his imagination and maps a course which includes most of Europe as it was known to the Greeks in his time, the third century before Christ. According to him, the *Argo* on its return voyage sailed from the Black Sea up the Danube to the arm of that river which flowed into the Adriatic (a common idea among the Greeks). Having followed this river to the Adriatic, the boat sails up the Po into the Rhone (the Alps are not mentioned), and then down the Rhone into the Mediterranean. The Argonauts then visit the home of Circe and the island of the Sirens, passing Scylla and Charybdis and the Clashing Rocks. They finally reach the land of the Phaeacians, but are driven by a storm to the northern coast of Africa. Here they carry the *Argo* overland to the Lake Tritonis. The god Triton shows them a passage from the lake into the Mediterranean, and they finally sail to Aegina and then to Pagasae in Thessaly. The account is entertaining, but it does not do justice even to the geographical knowledge of the period. The latter part of the story is, in fact, quite Homeric, introducing as it does imaginary places in the western Mediterranean which were visited by Odysseus.

It is obvious that the story of the Argonauts as we have it throws little light upon the state of geographical knowledge in any period.

IV. *Geography of the Homeric Poems*

THE *Iliad* and the *Odyssey* are the earliest documents that give us information on the subject of geography. They were written at a time when it was believed that the earth was flat, circular, and surrounded by the stream of the ocean which flowed around the earth. The sky was supposed to be a concave vault resting upon the circumference of the earth. In the *Odyssey*[1] Atlas is said to hold the pillars which keep earth and sky apart. The identification of Atlas with the mountain in northwestern Africa is much later, appearing first in Herodotus.[2] The three continents were not differentiated and named until the fifth century. In the *Hymn to the Pythian Apollo*[3] the name Europe is used of northern Greece. Aeschylus[4] first uses it of the whole continent, making the Phasis the boundary between Europe and Asia, and the Pillars of Hercules the boundary between Europe and Africa. In the *Iliad*[5] there is a reference to the Asiatic meadows of the Caÿster, but the term is apparently only a local designation. The earliest application of the name to the whole continent appears first in writers of the early part of the fifth century. The name Libya in the *Odyssey*[6] has a local meaning, referring to the part of Africa which is west of Egypt.

[1] i, 53–54.
[2] iv, 184.
[3] 250–251; 290–291.
[4] *Frag.*, 177.
[5] ii, 461.
[6] iv, 87; xiv, 295.

The author or authors of the Homeric poems appear to have had little definite geographical knowledge beyond Greece, the Aegean Sea, and western Asia Minor, although in the study of this subject it is never safe to assume that, because a writer does not mention a place, he has never heard of it. The most significant passages indicating geographical knowledge are, in the *Iliad*,[1] the catalogue of the Greek ships and the list of the Trojan forces, and, in the *Odyssey*, the long story of the wanderings of Odysseus [2] and the brief account of the voyage of Menelaus.[3] The Greek ships come from all parts of Greece except Epirus and Acarnania, from the islands west of Greece, and from those of the Aegean. The Trojan forces come from the region about Troy, from the opposite shore of Thrace, and from Asia Minor as far east as Paphlagonia.

The story of the travels of Odysseus on his return from Troy is one of the most interesting parts of the *Odyssey*, and is of geographical value, since it enables us to determine with some certainty the western limit of the geographical knowledge of the time. The ancient geographers located almost every place mentioned in the narrative, but many of their identifications are arbitrary and obviously impossible. Modern attempts to trace the voyage and locate the places are, at least in part, unconvincing.[4]

After leaving Troy Odysseus lands on the coast of Thrace among the Cicones,[5] an historical people men-

[1] ii, 484 ff.   [2] ix–xii.
[3] iii, 276 ff.   [4] W. Dörpfeld, *Homers Odyssee*,
[5] ix, 39.   pp. 249 ff.

tioned by Vergil and Ovid. From here he sails to
Cape Malea, but is driven from his course by the
north wind and carried for nine days across the sea
to the land of the Lotus-eaters, also an historical
people, living on the northern coast of Africa near the
Lesser Syrtis.[1] So far it may be assumed that the
account is based upon geographical knowledge.

From this point there are only occasional indica-
tions of distance or direction. All that can be said
with certainty is that the various places mentioned
appear to be west of Greece. Odysseus now sails to
the land of the Cyclopes,[2] which was located quite
arbitrarily by later writers on the eastern coast of
Sicily. The author of the *Odyssey* had heard of Sicily,
which was known to him as Sicania,[3] and the fact that
he does not say that the Cyclopes lived in Sicily is
some evidence that he did not intend to place them
there.

From the land of the Cyclopes Odysseus sails to the
island of Aeolus,[4] identified by the ancient geographers with one of the group north of Sicily called the
Aeolian Islands, an identification quite without justi-
fication, as there is no information regarding the
length or direction of the voyage. From here he sails
for nine days with a favoring west wind, and is in
sight of Ithaca when his mutinous sailors open the
bag of winds provided by Aeolus and the fleet is carried back to the island of Aeolus. From this statement it is obvious that the author regarded the island

[1] ix, 84.   [2] *Ibid.*, 106.
[3] xxiv, 307.   [4] x, 1.

of Aeolus and probably the land of the Cyclopes as lying a long distance west of Greece.

Leaving the island, Odysseus and his men row for six days and reach the land of the Laestrygones,[1] placed by the Greek geographers at one point or another in Sicily, by the Romans in Italy, near Formiae. There is nothing in the *Odyssey* to justify either location. But there is a curious statement that in this region the paths of night and day lie close together, meaning, perhaps, that the interval between nightfall and daybreak is very short — a statement due, possibly, to some vague rumor of the land of the midnight sun, which had been brought by traders from Britain to the Strait of Gibraltar or by those who came down the rivers of Scythia to the Black Sea.

From here the wanderers continue their journey to Aeaea, the island-home of Circe,[2] identified by later writers with a mountainous promontory on the coast of Latium, although it is described in the *Odyssey* as a low island with the boundless sea all about it. Next, with a favoring north wind they sail to the land of the Cimmerii,[3] who dwell beyond the stream of the ocean in a place of perpetual darkness. This statement is interesting and, possibly, significant. It suggests that though the Greeks of the time understood the stream of Oceanus to lie not far west of Sicily, they yet had some notion of inhabited land beyond. Except that the vessels sail with a favoring north wind and that the land of the Cimmerii is, therefore, south of the island of Circe, there is no indication of its position

[1] x, 82.   [2] *Ibid.*, 135.   [3] *Ibid.*, 507; xi, 13 ff.

and even the ancient writers made no attempt to locate it. The historical Cimmerii lived originally on the northern shore of the Black Sea and were said to have been driven out by the Scythians and then to have settled in Asia Minor. This can hardly have been the location in the mind of the author of the *Odyssey*.

Odysseus returns to Circe's island and starts for home.[1] He passes the island of the Sirens,[2] placed by ancient writers off the Campanian coast, avoids the so-called Clashing Rocks,[3] and sails between Scylla and Charybdis.[4] These were located by the geographers in the Strait of Messina, perhaps correctly, since the author of the *Odyssey* may have heard from Phoenician traders of the difficult passage between Italy and Sicily. The location would be certain if Thrinacia, the next landing-place, could be identified as either Sicily or southern Italy.

After the departure from Thrinacia a storm rises and Odysseus is carried on the wreck of his vessel back between Scylla and Charybdis and beyond, for nine days, until on the tenth he lands at Ogygia, the home of the nymph Calypso.[5] This is identified by some with a small rocky island off the coast of Bruttium, by others with an island near Malta. From here he sails on a raft for seventeen days toward the east (keeping the constellation of the Great Bear on his left), and on the following day sees the land of the Phaeacians.[6] This statement, added to the story of

---

[1] xii, 3 ff.   [2] *Ibid.*, 167.   [3] *Ibid.*, 61.
[4] *Ibid.*, 234 ff.   [5] *Ibid.*, 448.   [6] v, 269 ff.

the voyage eastward from the island of Aeolus, is sufficient evidence that the author regarded the adven-
tures of his hero as occurring in the western Mediterranean. When in sight of Scheria, the land of the
Phaeacians, the raft is wrecked, but three days later
Odysseus swims ashore. Scheria was thought by the
ancient writers to be Corcyra, but the identification
was doubted even in antiquity.

This story has perhaps been given in greater detail
than its geographical importance warrants. Except
the references to the country of the Lotus-eaters,
and possibly Scylla and Charybdis, there is no sure
indication in the narrative that the author had any
knowledge of places beyond the limits of the early
Greek world.

It is interesting to speculate on the idea that the
Argonautic expedition and the wanderings of Odysseus in their original form were confined to the eastern
Mediterranean, the Aegean, and the Black Sea; that,
as vague information of the western Mediterranean
came from Cretan or Phoenician traders, the scene of
a part of the stories was shifted, retaining, however,
reminiscences of the earlier form. For example, the
Clashing Rocks are placed by Homer and his imi-
tator, Apollonius Rhodius, somewhere in the western
Mediterranean; by Herodotus and others in the
Black Sea — a recurrence, perhaps, to an earlier version. The reference to the long days in the land of
the Laestrygones is the sort of story which in later
times was brought down to the Black Sea from the
far north. The island of Aeaea, though apparently in

the western Mediterranean, is said to be the dwelling of the early dawn, the place of the rising of the sun.[1] Finally, the Cimmerii, placed by Homer in the extreme south, or possibly west, are elsewhere a well-known people, living on the northern shore of the Black Sea.

Another journey of the *Odyssey* [2] is that of Menelaus, very briefly described, but extending the horizon of the author's geographical knowledge far to the east and south. Menelaus visits Cyprus, Phoenicia, Egypt, Libya, and even the Ethiopians; also a people called the Erembi, who are identified by Strabo [3] with the Arabians.

Besides the passages already mentioned there are in the *Iliad* and the *Odyssey* scattered allusions to places more or less remote. In the *Iliad* [4] there is a reference to several Scythian peoples, including the Mysians, interesting on account of the tradition that the Mysians of Asia Minor had migrated from that part of Europe which was known as Moesia. The Sidonians are mentioned several times in the *Iliad* and *Odyssey*, the Phoenicians only once in the former, several times in the latter. Egypt does not appear in the *Iliad*, with the exception of an allusion to the wealth of Thebes; [5] it is often mentioned in the *Odyssey*, and there are references to the Nile, which is called Aegyptos. In both works there are references to the Ethiopians, and there is even an allusion to the Pygmies, who lived on the shore of the southern ocean

[1] xii, 3. [2] iii, 276 ff.; iv, 83 ff. [3] i, 2, 34–35.
[4] xiii, 4–6. [5] ix, 381–384.

and fought with the cranes.[1] In the *Odyssey* [2] there is
a curious statement that the Ethiopians, the most
remote of peoples, are divided into two parts, those
living where the sun rises and those living where it
sets, but it can hardly be assumed from this that the
author had any conception of the width of the African continent. The Ethiopians of the East probably
lived near the Red Sea, and those of the West who
were known in Homer's time lived not far west of the
upper Nile.

In conclusion it may be said that, on the basis of
what is actually said in the *Iliad* and the *Odyssey*,
and disregarding possible differences in the date of
composition between the two works and among the
parts of either work, the world of Homer was bounded
on the north, very vaguely, by Scythian peoples; on
the east by the Black Sea, central Asia Minor, and
Phoenicia; on the south by the Ethiopians; and on
the west by Sicily. There is no evidence that the
author knew anything of the Asiatic continent east
of Phoenicia, nor does he mention Italy (unless
Thrinacia is southern Italy), the Phoenician settlements in the western Mediterranean, or the Pillars
of Hercules. He knew something of the African continent, but the Phoenicians and the Egyptians are
the only peoples outside the Aegean world concerning whom he had any definite information.

[1] *Il.*, iii, 3–6.   [2] i, 23–24.

V. *Geographical Progress between Homer and Hecataeus*

THE long period between Homer and the first published geography was marked by a considerable extension of the limits of the known world (if we may accept as evidence the geographical work ascribed to Hecataeus), but, especially, by the gradual acquisition of a much more complete knowledge of the coasts and islands of the Mediterranean Sea. During this period the Greeks were supplanting the Phoenicians as traders and colonizers. This process began in the West and, according to Strabo,[1] Cumae in Campania was the earliest Greek colony, coming from Chalcis in Euboea, the mother-city of many other colonies. It is difficult to accept the traditional date of its founding, 1050 years before Christ, in view of the fact that none of the other Greek colonies was earlier than the latter half of the eighth century. However that may be, Cumae was one of the most important of the colonies, being nearest to Rome and contributing most to its civilization. The neighboring Neapolis also was a Greek city, possibly a colony of Cumae, but its origin and the date of its founding are quite problematical.

If we can depend at all upon traditional dates, there was great activity in colonization toward the end of the eighth century. Among the earliest colonies were Naxos, Syracuse, and Megara on the eastern coast of Sicily; Sybaris, Croton, Metapontum, and Tarentum

[1] v, 4, 4.

in southern Italy. Tarentum was one of the few colonies of the Lacedaemonians. In the seventh and
sixth centuries other colonies were founded on the
coast of southern Italy and Sicily, and there were
many offshoots from the parent colonies. This whole
region became well known to the Greeks; indeed, it
became a part of the Greek world. These Greek ad-
venturers, however, are scarcely to be regarded as
real discoverers. It may be assumed that they had
from Phoenician traders some previous knowledge of
the regions to which they were going. It is curious,
however, that we have no information as to the fate
of the Phoenician settlements or the relations between
the Greeks and their predecessors.

Farther west, the Phocaeans from Asia Minor
founded Massilia about 600 years before Christ, in a
region then occupied by Ligurians, and Massilia sent
out colonies east and west and became a sort of Greek
outpost in the West. Regarding the Phocaeans,
Herodotus [1] has an interesting statement that they
were the earliest Greeks to make long sea-voyages;
that they discovered the Adriatic Sea, Tyrrhenia
(Etruria), Iberia (Spain), and Tartessus. He has another story [2] of a vessel from Samos which was driven
by the east wind between the Pillars of Hercules and
reached Tartessus, a place that had never before been
visited.

The Phoenicians were well established in Corsica,
Sardinia, and Spain, and there is no evidence that the
Greeks made any attempt to supplant them, though

[1] i, 163.   [2] iv, 152.

there is reason to think that for a time the Phocaeans were settled in Sardinia and on the eastern coast of Spain. This is true also of the northern coast of Africa from the Pillars of Hercules to the Syrtes. But between the Syrtes and Egypt there was a fertile region occupied only by native tribes, and here the Dorians from the island of Thera founded the important city of Cyrene. In Egypt the Ionians and Carians were permitted to settle on the west arm of the Nile at Naucratis, which became an important Greek trading-centre in the only part of the Delta which foreign vessels were allowed to enter.

The earliest historical settlements on the Euxine (the Black Sea) were somewhat later than those in the western Mediterranean, though there was a tradition of earlier colonies planted by the Carians. By the middle of the seventh century the Greeks had explored the sea and established colonies, first on the Propontis and the Bosphorus, and afterward on the north, west, and south shores of the Euxine. Many of these were founded by the Milesians, but Byzantium, the one that was destined to become the most important, was founded by the Megarians. These colonies developed rapidly and themselves established others. The Milesians especially seem to have realized the importance of settlements on the north coast as a means of trade with the interior, and for this purpose planted colonies at the mouths of the rivers and at the entrance to the Sea of Azov.

By the end of the sixth century the Greeks had become familiar with the whole Mediterranean including the Euxine. Through their colonies on the coasts they had probably gained some knowledge of the interior, — for example, of Gaul through Massilia, of central and southern Italy through the many Greek towns on the west and south coasts, of Scythia and Asia Minor through the colonies on the Euxine. They were probably well acquainted with the lower valley of the Nile and had learned a good deal from the Egyptians about the more remote parts of Egypt and about Ethiopia. Some knowledge of the more civilized peoples of the east they must already have acquired from both Egyptians and Phoenicians, with whom the eastern peoples had commercial relations at a very early time. There is no evidence that the Greeks themselves during this period journeyed to these remote regions or established trade relations with the peoples of the east, but the geography of Hecataeus and the writings of his immediate successors show some acquaintance with Persia, Arabia, and even with India.

The only author of this period whose writings are preserved in anything but fragmentary form is Hesiod, and his works are so largely interpolated with later additions that they are not dependable as indicating the geographical knowledge of the time. The following facts, however, may be noted. The rivers Eridanus, Phasis, and Ister (Danube), not mentioned in the Homeric poems, appear in the *Theogony*.[1] In the same work [2] the Hesperides are located beyond the stream of ocean, and the three-

[1] 337–445.   [2] 215–216, 287 ff.

headed Geryones is said to live on the island Erythea, beyond Oceanus. In the *Works and Days* [1] there is a similar statement regarding the Islands of the Blessed. It is possible that when these passages were written the Greeks had already heard of the Madeira or Canary Islands in the Atlantic Ocean off the northwestern coast of Africa. There is no reference in Hesiod to Italy or Sicily except a curious passage in the *Theogony* [2] in which the writer says that Latinus, son of Odysseus and Circe, rules over the Tyrrhenians in the distant recesses of the Sacred Islands. Later writers [3] speak of Hesiod as knowing Aetna, Ortygia, the Ligurians, Scythians, and Ethiopians, but there is no evidence of this in the poems as we have them.

An early work of some geographical interest was an epic poem written by Aristeas of Proconnesus, an island in the Propontis. It was quoted as late as Pausanias,[4] but only a few fragments survive. It is interesting because it treated the more or less fabulous tribes living north of the Euxine and shows that the Greeks were beginning to realize the great extent of the country between the Euxine and the northern ocean.

During this period between Homer and the earliest geographer, the physical philosophers, especially Thales, Anaximander, and Anaximenes, were engaged in speculations concerning the physical phenomena of the universe and doubts were expressed

[1] 171.   [2] 1013–1016.
[3] Strabo, i, 2, 14; vii, 3, 7.   [4] i, 24, 6.

THE WORLD ACCORDING TO HECATAEUS

as to the flatness of the earth. Anaximander is said
to have made the first map of the earth's surface.[1]
Before the end of the sixth century Pythagoras was
teaching his pupils that the earth was a sphere.

VI. *Hecataeus*

THE credit of writing the first geography has usually
been given to the historian Hecataeus of Miletus, but
even in antiquity his claim to that distinction was
questioned, and it must be admitted that the work
ascribed to him is of somewhat doubtful authorship.[2]
Herodotus and Aristotle say nothing about it and
Athenaeus [3] says that Callimachus, the librarian at
Alexandria, ascribes it to Nesiotes. On the other
hand, Eratosthenes, the geographer of the third century, accepts the authorship of Hecataeus, and, according to Strabo,[4] says that the work is believed to
be his on account of its similarity to his other writings. Only small fragments [5] survive, and they are
chiefly mere names quoted by Stephanus of Byzantium. However, on the assumption that Hecataeus
was in fact the author, they are sufficient to give a
good idea of the extent of the world as it was known
to the Greeks at the end of the sixth century. There
are of course many gaps in our knowledge of the
work, and it must be remembered that the fact that
a place is not mentioned in the extant fragments is
not a proof that the author did not know it.

[1] Eratosthenes, in Strabo, i, 1, 11.
[2] See especially J. Wells, in *Journal of Hellenic Studies*, vol. XXIX (1909).
[3] ii, 70.   [4] i, 1, 11.   [5] Jacoby, *Frag. Gr. Hist.*

The work was a *periodos* in two books of the Mediterranean Sea and the seas opening into it. In the first book the northern coasts of the Mediterranean and the Euxine were described from Tartessus, outside the Pillars of Hercules, to the Caucasus Mountains. There is no reference to the western coast of Spain beyond Tartessus. The author mentions Corsica, Sardinia, Capreae, and the iron mines of Aethale (Elba); also, Massilia and Monoecus on the Ligurian coast, and Narbo, which he calls a Celtic city. There are references not only to the Greek towns on the coast of southern Italy, but to those of the Oenotrians in the interior. No town in Italy farther north than Capua is mentioned and there is no reference to Latium or Etruria, though the Greeks of Campania must have known the towns of Latium and certainly had trade relations with the Etruscans. The author evidently knew the east coast of the Adriatic, including Istria. In eastern Europe he mentions several tribes and cities of the Scythians, but none of the Greek cities on the Euxine.

The second book contained a description of the Asiatic and African coasts from the Caucasus Mountains to Thinge (later Tingis) outside the Pillars of Hercules, and gave also a good deal of information about the interior. The author appears to have regarded the Cimmerian Bosphorus and the river Tanais as the boundary between Europe and Asia. His information about Asia is rather surprising and might be taken as evidence of a later date for the work if Herodotus, writing in the middle of the fifth century, did not show a much more extensive and detailed knowledge. He mentions many cities of Asia Minor, Persia, Phoenicia, and Arabia; the Colchi and the Moschi east of the Euxine; the Caspian Sea, which he calls also the Hyrcanian, and the river Araxes flowing into it; the Parthians south of the Caspian and the Chorasmii to the east; the Persian Gulf. The names of India and the river Indus first appear in this work. There are references to several tribes and cities of India, especially the Gandarae or Gandarii, with their city Caspapyrus. In Africa, besides giving the cities on the north coast, the author apparently described Egypt in some detail, including the customs of the people.

VII. *The Voyage of Hanno*

ONE of the most picturesque incidents in the history of ancient geography is the voyage of Hanno, a Carthaginian, along the western coast of Africa. As the name was a very common one at Carthage, it is impossible to identify this Hanno and there is, moreover, no way of determining the date of the expedition. The most probable date appears to lie somewhere between 500 and 480 years before Christ. The story of the voyage was inscribed on a tablet in the temple of Moloch at Carthage, and a Greek translation of this was known to Aristotle. A copy of the Greek translation still exists at Heidelberg.[1] It must be admitted that the description of the voyage is very unsatisfactory. Most of the places mentioned cannot

[1] Mueller, *Geographi Graeci Minores*, vol. i.

be located and the southernmost limit, though much discussed, remains quite doubtful. And yet, because the expedition traveled seas hitherto unknown and visited lands not before trodden by civilized man, its contribution to the discovery of the ancient world was of very great importance.

Since the purpose of the expedition was colonization, not exploration, there were probably many vessels in the fleet, but the number given — 60 ships and 30,000 men and women — seems incredible. According to the narrative the first colony was planted at Thymiaterium, two days' sail outside the Pillars of Hercules. Then, sailing toward the west, the voyagers came to a promontory called Soloeis, the Promunturium Solis of Pliny's *Natural History*.[1] Here they turned toward the east and in half a day reached a point where there was, not far from the sea, a lake or marsh, near which were many elephants. In the course of one day's sail beyond this point they left five groups of colonists. Sailing on (the distance is not given), they came to the river Lixus (probably the river Draa). Here they found friendly natives, who told them that in the interior there were high mountains, hostile Ethiopians, and cave-dwellers. From here they sailed for two days toward the south and one day toward the east and came to a bay containing a small island. Here they founded the town of Cerne, which became an important city for trade with tribes of the interior. The exact location cannot be determined, though Hanno in his narrative says that

[1] v, 1.

it was as far from the Pillars of Hercules as they were from Carthage, that is, approximately 900 English miles. His reckoning, however, was necessarily quite vague, since it was based only upon the number of days consumed in the voyage. In the *periplus* ascribed to Scylax,[1] Cerne is located seven days' voyage from Soloeis and twelve from the Pillars of Hercules. Ptolemy [2] puts it in 25° 40′ north latitude. There is no agreement among modern investigators. In this connection Hanno makes the curious statement that Cerne was opposite Carthage, which can only be interpreted as meaning that it was directly south of Carthage. Though it is difficult to understand how he could have made such a blunder, he must have thought, if this is what he actually wrote, that his course beyond the promontory Soloeis was generally southeast or east rather than southwest. This explanation is corroborated by the later geographers, who thought that the western coast of Africa, beginning at a point near the Pillars of Hercules, extended toward the southeast. On the other hand the directions as given in Hanno's narrative do not support this statement, and it may be that the Greek translator misunderstood the Phoenician text.

From Cerne two voyages were made. First, the vessels sailed up a great river into a lake, in which there were three islands. On the other side were high mountains, and wild people, who threw stones at the travelers and prevented their landing. Having made their way back to the coast, they went on to another

[1] 112 (53).   [2] iv, 6, 33.

large river full of crocodiles and hippopotami. This has generally been identified with the Senegal. After returning to Cerne, they sailed south for twelve days to a headland usually identified with Cape Verde. It took them two days to round this promontory. Beyond was a bay, perhaps the mouth of the Gambia, surrounded by a plain where they saw fires flashing at night. From here they went on for five days to a great gulf, which, according to interpreters accompanying the expedition, was called the Western Horn. In this gulf was an island, where they landed. Then they sailed on for four days past a region that was full of fire, where blazing torrents poured into the sea, until they reached a flaming mountain, which was called Theon Ochema, the Chariot of the Gods. A voyage of three days from here brought them to a bay, which was named the Southern Horn and is often identified with Sherboro Sound. Here, on an island, they found men and women covered with hair, called by the interpreters gorillas. This was the southern limit of the expedition, which was forced to return because of lack of supplies.

This is the narrative of Hanno. There has been much discussion regarding the location of places mentioned in the Greek text and, especially, as to the point finally reached. If we may depend upon the statements in the text, it was a voyage of twenty-six days from Cerne to the Southern Horn, but, as we do not know with certainty the location of Cerne and as a day's voyage was of greatly varying length, we cannot on that basis reach any very satisfactory result.

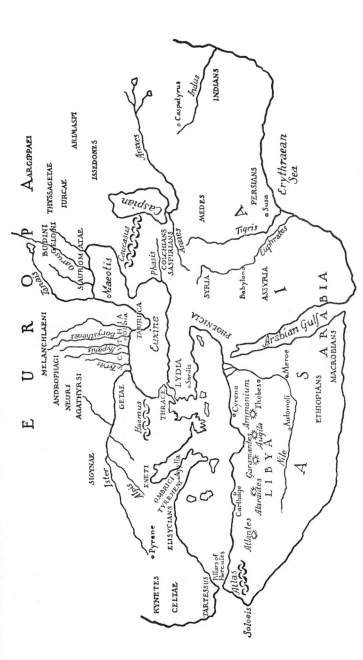

THE WORLD ACCORDING TO HERODOTUS

Sherboro Sound is in 7° 45' north latitude, but many think that the expedition did not go nearly so far south. In any case, this was for many centuries the limit of geographical knowledge of the western coast of Africa. No ancient navigator went farther than Hanno, and his expedition represents the sum of Ptolemy's knowledge of this part of the world in the second century after Christ.

VIII. *Herodotus*

WITH the exception of Herodotus the writers of the fifth century give us little geographical information. The fragments of the *Prometheus Unbound* of Aeschylus show that in that play he described the journey of Heracles from the Caucasus Mountains to the Hesperides, and there are references to the Erythraean Sea (the Indian Ocean) and to the Ligurians. The scene of the *Persae* of Aeschylus is laid at Susa and there are references to Babylon and Ecbatana, to the Parthians, Mardians, and Bactrians, — places and peoples made familiar to the Greeks by the recent expedition of Xerxes. Pindar's account [1] of the Argonautic expedition has already been mentioned, and he has also a description of the land of the Hyperboreans.[2] There are a few fragments of a *periplus* by Damastes of Sigeum,[3] probably a contemporary of Herodotus, to whom is ascribed the earliest reference to Rome.

[1] *Pyth.*, iv.   [2] *Olymp.*, iii, 14–31; *Pyth.*, x, 30–44.
[3] Jacoby, *Frag. Gr. Hist.*

Though Herodotus was primarily a historian, he was apparently very much interested in geography and gives an excellent description of the world as it was known to the Greeks in the fifth century before Christ. He was a great traveler and his credibility is enhanced by the fact that he himself had visited many of the places which he describes. He knew by personal observation not only Greece, the Greek islands, and the coast of Asia Minor, but he had probably gone up the Nile to the first cataract (125 miles above Thebes) and had visited Cyrene, Babylon, Olbia at the mouth of the river Borysthenes, and Colchis. In the latter part of his life he joined a colony sent by the Athenians to Thurii in southern Italy, where he died. The idea of traveling for the purpose of recreation or observation was, so far as we know, a new thing in his time, due, no doubt, to increased safety and convenience of transportation, and must henceforth have contributed largely to the development and dissemination of geographical knowledge. There are, of course, many mistakes in Herodotus, but the extent of his information is astonishing. It must be remembered, however, that the work of Hecataeus is fragmentary and that we have here the first detailed record of the advance that had been made in many directions in the discovery of the world.

Herodotus believed that Europe was larger than Asia and Africa together and reached this conclusion by assuming that it extended all the way from the western ocean to the eastern, if there was an eastern ocean; that is, the eastern part of Europe was north of Asia as the western part was north of Africa.[1] The boundary between Europe and Asia was the Euxine, the river Phasis, the Caspian, and the river Iaxartes (which he calls the Araxes). He believed also that Europe was wider from north to south than Asia and Africa.[2] However, he says that nobody knows anything about northern and eastern Europe, not even whether they are bounded by the sea.[3]

His description of Asia is peculiar.[4] He says that there are four nations extending from south to north, — Persians (including the Indians), Medes, Saspirians (living in eastern Armenia), and Colchians. Asia, he says, has two projections toward the west, — Asia Minor (not so called, however, until the fifth century after Christ) and, secondly, the region between the Erythraean Sea and the Mediterranean, this being occupied by Assyrians, Syrians, Phoenicians, and Arabians. But, he says, the Arabian Gulf (the Red Sea) is not the end; and he goes on to include all Africa in this second projection.

Libya (that is, Africa), according to Herodotus, is surrounded by the sea, and, since he believes that Arabia extends farthest to the south of all inhabited countries,[5] it is clear that he thinks of the south coast of Africa as extending to the west or northwest from a point near the entrance of the Arabian Gulf to Soloeis on the western coast. This is the conception also of later geographers, who knew nothing of the great southern part of the African continent. To

---

[1] iv, 42, 45.   [2] *Ibid.*, 42   [3] iii, 115.
[4] iv, 37–39.   [5] iii, 107.

prove his point that Libya is surrounded by water, Herodotus tells an interesting story.[1] When Necho was king of Egypt, in the seventh or sixth century before Christ, an expedition started in the Arabian Gulf, made the circuit of Africa, and returned in the third year through the Pillars of Hercules. It stopped on the way at least once to raise grain. Herodotus believes the tale to be true, but does not accept the statement that when the expedition was sailing along the southern coast it had the sun on the right. That is, he somewhat naïvely rejects a detail which was a strong argument for the truth of the story. It is strange, moreover, that he questions this, for Meroe on the Nile and most of the Indian Ocean are south of the Tropic of Cancer and the phenomenon must have been more or less familiar at the time. This story, if true, is evidence of a very early interest in exploration for its own sake, an interest that Herodotus himself manifests perhaps more than any other Greek writer. He tells another story of an attempt to circumnavigate Africa.[2] A Persian nobleman, Sataspes, was condemned to death by Xerxes, but the sentence was remitted on condition that he sail around Africa. He sailed west from Egypt through the Pillars of Hercules and a long distance south of the promontory of Soloeis. He was forced to return and was executed.

This is the general conception of Herodotus regarding the extent and outline of the world, but he gives very many details which have not appeared in any earlier source.

[1] iv, 42.   [2] Ibid., 43.

He obviously had no idea of the western coast of
Europe. Tartessus he regards as a district of southern
Spain.[1] He speaks of the Celts as living beyond the
Pillars of Hercules, and the Kynetes (a name unknown to later geographers) as living beyond the
Celts.[2] He mentions the Elisycians,[3] who lived between the Pyrenees and the Rhone and appear in
Hecataeus as a Ligurian tribe. The Tyrrhenians
(Etruscans) he regards as a formidable naval power,
originating in Lydia, and refers especially to Agylla,
which was afterward called Caere.[4] Rome he does
not mention. He does not know the Alps, but speaks
of the Alpis as a river flowing from the country north
of the Ombrici (Umbrians) into the Danube.[5] The
latter, he says, rises near the town of Pyrene in the
land of the Celts, flows through the middle of Europe,
and, on account of its tributaries, fifteen of which he
enumerates, is the greatest of all rivers.[6] The country north of the Danube, he says, is mostly unknown;
he mentions only the Sigynae, whose land extends as
far as that of the Eneti on the Adriatic.[7] He knows
Mount Haemus [8] (the Balkans), and includes the
Getae in Thrace, treating that country as larger than
it appears to be in the later geographers.[9]

Herodotus had surprisingly incorrect ideas about
the size of the Euxine and the sea called Maeotis (the
Sea of Azov), especially the latter.[10] His only basis of
reckoning was days' journeys by water. He exagger-

[1] i, 163.   [2] ii, 33; iv, 49.   [3] vii, 165.
[4] i, 94, 166–167.   [5] iv, 49.   [6] Ibid., 48–49; ii, 33.
[7] v, 9.   [8] iv, 49.
[9] Ibid., 93.   [10] Ibid., 85–86.

ates enormously the length of the Euxine and says
that the Maeotis is nearly as large as the Euxine. It
is in reality about one-twelfth as large. This misconception persisted in later writers. He does not know
that the isthmus connecting the Tauric peninsula
with the mainland is only about five miles wide. He
compares the peninsula with Attica and Iapygia,[1]
whereas he might better have compared it with the
Peloponnesus, which, moreover, is of about the same
size.

He gives much information about the Scythians
and other peoples occupying the great region north
of the Euxine and the Caucasus Mountains. The
Greeks living in the colonies on the Euxine had
learned about this country from traders who went
back and forth on the rivers which flow into that sea.
They had been interested also in the expedition of
Darius toward the end of the sixth century. Herodotus tells[2] how that monarch with 700,000 men
crossed the Bosphorus and marched through Thrace
to the Danube. Having crossed that river, he pur-
sued the Scythians in a northeasterly direction to the
Tanais. On the other side he penetrated the lands of
the Sauromatae and the Budini as far as the river
Oarus, which has sometimes been identified as the
Volga. He now turned to the west, entered the countries of the Melanchlaeni, Androphagi, Neuri, and
Agathyrsi, and, finally, with a small remnant of his
army, retreated to the Danube. There are some incredible things in the story and, according to Strabo,[3]

[1] iv, 99.   [2] Ibid., 120–142.   [3] vii, 3, 14.

Darius never reached even the river Tyras. But, whatever may be the truth of his narrative, Herodotus shows a somewhat surprising knowledge of this region.

Scythia itself he limits quite definitely to a region about 400 miles square north of the Euxine and west of the Maeotis.[1] That is, he regards the Scythians as a distinct people, whereas some of the geographers apply the name indiscriminately to all the peoples of northern Europe and Asia. He describes, not always correctly, the rivers Tyras (Dniester), Hypanis [2] (Bug), Borysthenes [3] (Dnieper), and Tanais [4] (Don), and mentions others which cannot be identified.[5] He gives much information,[6] not only about the Scythians, but about other peoples living to the north and east, some of them more or less fabulous: the highly civilized Agathyrsi; the Neuri, who were able to transform themselves into wolves; the Androphagi, the only cannibals of this part of the world; the Melanchlaeni; the Budini; the Geloni, who were originally Greeks and had temples dedicated to Greek gods; and, farther south, the Sauromatae, who afterward crossed the Tanais and occupied what is now central and western Russia. Other peoples, the Thyssagetae and the Iurcae,[7] he describes as living in a fertile plain beyond the Budini. Farther to the east were the Argippaei,[8] living in the foothills of high mountains, probably the Urals. So far, says Herod-

[1] iv, 99. [2] Ibid., 51–52. [3] Ibid., 53.
[4] Ibid., 57. [5] Ibid., 54–56, 123. [6] Ibid., 104 ff.
[7] Ibid., 22. [8] Ibid., 23.

otus,[1] the country is well known from traders. Beyond this, there were only vague reports of other peoples to the north or east, — men with goats' feet, living in the mountains; others who slept for six months in the year (an interesting indication of rumors from the far north); the Issedones;[2] and the one-eyed Arimaspi.[3]

Regarding the Caspian Sea Herodotus was more correctly informed than some later geographers. He describes it[4] as an inland sea, with its greatest length from north to south, whereas others, centuries later, supposed that it was an inlet from the northern ocean and that its greatest length was from east to west.

Herodotus makes it clear that much of the continent of Asia south of the Euxine, the Caspian, and the river Iaxartes, and as far east as the Indus was now well known to the Greeks. This knowledge had come to them largely through their relations with the Persians during the reign of Darius. It may be noted that this energetic monarch sent out one of the few expeditions of antiquity whose sole purpose was exploration. By his orders Scylax of Caryanda, in Caria, had sailed down the Indus to the sea, and then, turning to the west, had gone on to the head of the Arabian Gulf, a voyage of thirty months.[5]

On account of his misconception of the length of the Euxine Herodotus makes Asia Minor too long and, also, he makes it too narrow.[6] He is well informed regarding the political organization of the Persian Empire, gives a list of twenty provinces,[7]

[1] iv, 24.   [2] *Ibid.*, 25.   [3] *Ibid.*, 27.   [4] i, 203.
[5] iv, 44.   [6] i, 72; ii, 34.   [7] iii, 90–94.

and describes the royal road from Sardis to Susa.[1] Strangely enough he has an idea that the river Indus flows toward the east.[2] India he treats as a part of Persia, and he has gathered a good deal of information about the extent, population, and products of the country. Caspatyrus (called Caspapyrus by Hecataeus) is the only town that he mentions.[3] East of India, he says,[4] there is nothing but uninhabited desert. He says nothing about the Persian Gulf, and speaks of the Tigris and Euphrates as flowing into the Erythraean Sea, which, he says, extends from the mouth of the Indus to the Arabian Gulf.[5]

Concerning Africa, Herodotus has far more information than any earlier writer. He believes that in its upper course the Nile flows from west to east and says that it is parallel with the Ister (the Danube), the one dividing Africa, the other Europe, and that the mouths of the two rivers are opposite each other.[6] He probably thought that the Ister turned to the southeast before entering the Euxine. This conception of the upper part of the Nile is based partly upon the following story, which Herodotus had heard at Cyrene.[7] Five young men from a tribe living near the Greater Syrtis crossed the desert toward the southwest and were captured by small black men, who took them to their native town. Past this flowed from west to east a large river filled with crocodiles. The young men had probably reached the Niger, but Herodotus thought that it was the Nile. There was

---

[1] v, 52–54.   [2] iv, 44.   [3] iii, 102; iv, 44.   [4] iii, 48; iv, 40.
[5] i, 189, 180; ii, 11.   [6] ii, 33–34.   [7] Ibid., 32–33.

much speculation in antiquity as to the source of the Nile. Ptolemy,[1] in the second century after Christ, was the first to state the fact that it rises in two lakes south of the equator. Herodotus describes the river in detail and with approximate correctness as far south as Meroe, the capital of the Ethiopians.[2] Farther up he mentions only a people whom he calls the Deserters, who, he says, live as far from Meroe as that city is from Elephantine.[3] Also, he tells the story of the expedition of Cambyses against the long-lived (Macrobian) Ethiopians, who lived somewhere southeast of Meroe.[4]

Herodotus was well informed about the northern coast of Africa as far as Carthage, though he seems to be ignorant of the Lesser Syrtis and thinks that the coast is straighter than it actually is.[5] He says little about the Carthaginians beyond speaking of their trade with people living outside the Pillars of Hercules.[6] In the interior he describes a succession of five oases extending along the northern border of the desert from a point not far from Thebes to Mount Atlas, which, he says, is a ridge extending beyond the Pillars of Hercules.[7] On the western coast he mentions only the promontory of Soloeis, which, he says, is the westernmost point of Africa.[8]

---

[1] iv, 8, 24.   [2] ii, 29.   [3] *Ibid.*, 30.
[4] iii, 17 ff., 25.   [5] ii, 32, 150.   [6] iv, 196.
[7] *Ibid.*, 181 ff.   [8] ii, 32; iv, 43.

IX. *Geographical Progress between Herodotus and Alexander*

DURING the century following Herodotus, though there was much writing on the subject, there was little increase in geographical knowledge, and most of the written works are no longer in existence. At the end of the fifth century the expedition of Cyrus against his brother Artaxerxes and the publication of the *Anabasis* of Xenophon added some details to the information possessed by the Greeks, though they were already familiar with much of the continent of Asia as far as the Tigris and Euphrates. And yet, in spite of the straightforwardness of the narrative, the *Anabasis*, from a geographical point of view, could hardly have been very instructive. There is a clear account of the early part of the expedition, from Sardis through Asia Minor and as far as Cunaxa on the Euphrates; that is, through country that was already pretty well known. From that point, however, as the Greeks who had been in the army of Cyrus marched northward, the narrative of Xenophon presents many difficulties. They probably crossed the Tigris at Sittace and went up the left bank to the river Zapatas. Beyond this, as they advanced through a hilly or mountainous region, ultimately reaching the snow-covered mountains of Armenia and descending to Trapezus on the Euxine, it is difficult, if not impossible, to follow their course and identify the places mentioned by Xenophon. That is, where clear statement is most needed, the writer is obscure and the *Anabasis* can scarcely have contributed much to the knowledge of this unfamiliar region.

Contemporary with Xenophon was Ctesias of Cnidus, who lived for many years at the Persian court as the physician of King Artaxerxes. His description of India is not extant, but we have a full summary of it in the work of Photius, written in the ninth century after Christ. Ignorance and credulity appear to have been the outstanding features of his work. He thought that India was as large as all the rest of Asia and accepted all the extravagant fables that were told about the people and customs of the country.

Ephorus and Theopompus, historians of the fourth century, whose works are not extant, included geographical material. Ephorus [1] in his thirty books of general history gave one book to the geography of Europe and one to that of Asia and Africa. Theopompus [2] in his *Philippica* spoke of the capture of Rome by the Gauls and in the fragments there are references to the Veneti, Umbrians, and Etruscans. The Greeks were apparently beginning to be interested in northern Italy.

The earliest geographical work surviving in complete form (except the narrative of Hanno's voyage) is the *Periplus* of Scylax,[3] which is ascribed in some manuscripts to Scylax of Caryanda, whom Darius sent on a voyage of exploration, but, on the basis of

[1] Mueller, *Frag. Hist. Graec.*, vol. i.   [2] *Ibid.*
[3] Mueller, *Geog. Graec. Min.*, vol. i.

internal evidence, is clearly of much later date, probably of the time of Philip of Macedon. The work is a *periplus* of the Mediterranean Sea, starting from the Pillars of Hercules and following the northern coast to the river Tanais, which is considered the boundary between Europe and Asia; and then following the coast of Asia and Africa back to the Pillars of Hercules. It includes also a description of the western coast of Africa as far as Cerne, and a list of twenty islands in the order of size. Since the work treats only that part of the world which had been for some time fairly well known, it shows little advance in geographical knowledge.

There are, however, some interesting details, especially concerning Italy. The Ligurians are said to extend from the mouth of the Rhone to Antipolis, that is, Antibes (the manuscripts say Antium, but that is obviously impossible); the Etruscans from there to Rome; the Latins to the Circeian promontory; the Volscians for a short distance; then the Campanians, the Samnites, and the Lucanians to the Sicilian strait. The Arno and the Tiber are not mentioned and, except a mere reference to Rome, no city is mentioned between Antipolis and the Campanians. After giving a complete list of the Greek cities in southern Italy and Sicily, the author describes the Adriatic coast of Italy, which had probably at a very early time attracted Greek traders.[1] He mentions the Iapygians, the Samnites, the Umbrians (with a reference to An-

---

[1] See Lysias, *Or.*, xxxii, 25; and, for a reference to the Veneti, Euripides, *Hippol.*, 231, 1131.

cona), the Etruscans, whose domain is said to extend from sea to sea, the Gauls, and the Veneti (with a reference to the river Eridanus). The account of the eastern coast of the Adriatic is detailed, but somewhat obscure. A statement about the river Ister in the land of the Istri shows that the author had the prevailing notion that a branch of the Danube flowed into the Adriatic.

In the description of Greece there is a puzzling statement to the effect that Arcadia has a coast-line between Elis and Messenia. The account of the northern coast of Africa from Egypt to Carthage is excellent; beyond that it is very meagre. Soloeis, on the western coast, is said to be five days' voyage from the Pillars of Hercules, Cerne seven days farther. Between Soloeis and Cerne there is a reference to the river Xion, probably the Lixus of Hanno. Beyond Cerne, according to the author, the sea is not navigable, but may extend to Egypt.

Plato, Aristotle, and the other philosophers of the fourth century contributed little to the subject of geography. In the *Timaeus* and the *Critias* [1] Plato gives his description of the mythical island Atlantis, which is said to be larger than Asia and Africa together and to fill most of the sea beyond the Pillars of Hercules. Aristotle was interested in speculations as to the nature of the universe and its phenomena, and offered several new arguments to prove the spherical shape of the earth.[2] He accepted the conclusion of certain mathematicians that the circumference was

[1] *Timaeus*, 5, 6; *Critias*, 3, 8.   [2] *De Caelo*, ii, 14, 13.

400,000 stadia, about 50,000 miles.[1] He ridiculed the
prevailing idea that the inhabited world — Europe,
Asia, and Africa — was round,[2] and was the first to
suggest that there was a habitable zone in the southern hemisphere.[3] There is a curious passage of some
geographical interest in the *Meteorologica*.[4] Parnasos,
he says, meaning Parapanisus, is the largest mountain toward the southeast, and there rise the greatest
rivers of Asia, the Araxes (that is, the Iaxartes), of
which the Tanais is a branch, and the Indus. Toward
the northeast, the Caucasus is the largest mountain,
from which also flow many large rivers. (He was us-
ing his imagination here; the Phasis is the only one
and that is small.) Pyrene is a mountain in the west,
in the Celtic country, and from this flow the Istrus
and the Tartessus, the former into the Euxine, the
latter into the sea beyond the Pillars of Hercules.
Most of the northern rivers rise in the Arcynian
Mountains. The Rhipaean Mountains are beyond
the limits of Scythia, and from these other large
rivers flow.

Dicaearchus, a pupil of Aristotle, wrote several
geographical works, including a general description
of the world, of which only a few fragments remain.
His maps were still in existence in Cicero's time.[5]

[1] *De Caelo*, ii, 14, 16.   [2] *Meteorolog.*, ii, 5, 13.   [3] *Ibid.*, 5, 16.
[4] i, 13, 15–22.   [5] Cic., *ad Att.*, vi, 2.

X. *Alexander and his Successors*

THE expedition of Alexander, one of the most astonishing achievements in history, gave to the western
world its first precise knowledge of the Far East. All
contemporary narratives of the expedition have disappeared, including the writings of the engineers and
surveyors who accompanied the army, and whose
works would have been exceedingly valuable for the
study of geography. The best existing account is by
Arrian, historian, geographer, and philosopher of the
second century after Christ, who based his narrative
upon the writings of Aristobulus and Ptolemy, who
accompanied Alexander. There is another account in
Strabo and information also in Diodorus, Plutarch,
and Q. Curtius, much of it based upon Clitarchus, a
contemporary of Alexander.

The expedition crossed the Hellespont in 334 B.C.
It is unnecessary to follow the line of march of the
conquering Macedonian host in its erratic course that
covered a large part of Asia Minor. After the battle
of Issus and the capture of Tyre and Gaza in Phoenicia, Alexander entered Egypt and went up the Nile
to Memphis. He then marched toward the west along
the coast to Paraetonium, and then toward the south
a journey of eight days to the oracle of Ammon in the
desert. On his return to Egypt he founded Alexandria
between Lake Mareotis and the sea. In the spring
of 331, having returned to Phoenicia, the expedition
proceeded toward the northeast through Syria,
crossed the Euphrates at Thapsacus, and, after mak-

ing a long detour to the north, crossed the Tigris into Assyria. After the defeat of Darius near Arbela and the capture of Babylon and Susa, the march was continued to the southeast to Persepolis. From this point, more or less continuously during a period of seven years, the expedition moved through regions little known or absolutely unknown, a distance of more than 7,000 miles, until in 324 Alexander with a part of his forces returned to Persepolis. A brief statement of the line of march will be sufficient. From Persepolis the expedition moved northwest to Ecbatana and then east to the Caspian Gates and Hecatompylos, not far from the southern shore of the Caspian Sea. After a long detour to the west Alexander began his amazing march into the unknown East. No other European has ever led an army into this part of the world, and the information secured by the members of this expedition constituted for centuries the geographical knowledge of this vast region. The army marched east through Parthia to Artacoana, and then south to Prophthasia, the principal city of Drangiana; then east and northeast through Arachosia to the Caucasus Mountains (the Hindu Kush). Some Greek geographers thought these a continuation of the mountains of the same name in Europe; others regarded them as a part of the Taurus ranges and called them Parapanisus.

In the spring of 329 Alexander crossed the mountains and proceeded west to Bactra, the chief city of Bactria or Bactriana; then, having crossed the great river Oxus, he went on through Sogdiana to the

Iaxartes, which flows into the Sea of Aral. This is the river which is sometimes called the Araxes, the one of which, according to Aristotle, the Tanais is a branch; in fact, when the Macedonians reached the Iaxartes, they thought that it was the Tanais.[1] This was the farthest point north reached by Alexander, and in this region he remained for some months subduing the peoples of Sogdiana and Bactriana.

The mountains to the east formed an impassable barrier, and so, after his long stay by the Iaxartes, he turned back to the south and from Bactra started on his march to India. He crossed the Indus and entered the Punjab, crossed the Hydaspes, and advanced as far as the Hyphasis or the Hesydrus. He intended to go on to the Ganges, but the discontent of his army forced him to return to the Hydaspes. Here a fleet was built and he embarked for the trip of nearly a thousand miles to Pattala near the mouth of the Indus, leaving a large part of the army to make the journey by land. During the voyage, which took nine months, he left colonies here and there, but all traces of Greek civilization soon disappeared and no one in antiquity added anything to the knowledge of the Indus brought back by the followers of Alexander.

For the return journey from Pattala to the west the forces were divided into three parts. Alexander himself with one section went through Gedrosia and Carmania into Persia. Another section followed a route farther north through Arachosia and Drangiana into Carmania. Nearchus with the fleet of 150 ships sailed

[1] Arrian, iii, 30; Strabo, xi, 7, 4.

from the mouth of the Indus to the head of the Persian Gulf. This voyage, which lasted five months, was generally regarded in antiquity as the first on the Indian Ocean, that of Scylax being disbelieved or forgotten. Nearchus himself wrote an account of it and of this there is a full abstract in Arrian.[1] Most of the places mentioned along the coast can be identified. Having reached the entrance of the Persian Gulf, he went ashore and had a conference with Alexander, who was then in Carmania. He then reëmbarked and continued the voyage to the head of the gulf. The land-forces and sea-forces were united at Susa. This was in 324. In the following year Alexander went to Babylon, intending to make it his capital. There is an interesting list of envoys who met him on that occasion; [2] they came from the following peoples: Libyans, Ethiopians, Scythians, Carthaginians, Bruttians, Lucanians, Tyrrhenians, Gauls, and Iberians. Pliny,[3] on the authority of Clitarchus, says that envoys came also from Rome. At the time of his death Alexander was planning the circumnavigation and conquest of Arabia.

Alexander did more than any other man of antiquity to extend geographical knowledge. His successors contributed little. Seleucus, who established himself at Babylon in 312 B.C. as monarch of all Asia, sent an expedition under Patrocles to explore the Caspian Sea [4] and undertook the conquest of northern India, but ultimately formed friendly relations with

---

[1] *Indica*, xxi ff.; Pliny, *N. H.*, vi, 26.   [2] Arrian, vii, 15; Diod., xvii, 113.
[3] *N. H.*, iii, 5 57.   [4] Strabo, xi, 7, 2 ff.

King Sandrocottus and sent Megasthenes as envoy
to his court at Palibothra (the modern Patna) on the
Ganges. Megasthenes was probably the first Greek
to reach the Ganges. He wrote a book,[1] of which
Arrian and Strabo have preserved considerable extracts, giving an account of his journey from the
Hyphasis, and describing Palibothra and the people
and products of that region. He described also,
though incorrectly, the route from Palibothra to the
mouth of the Ganges and gave the earliest information about the island Taprobane (Ceylon), though
its name was known to the companions of Alexander.[2]

The commercial activity of Alexandria added constantly to the definite knowledge of the Red Sea and
its coasts, Arabia, and India, though at this time
there was probably no direct trade between Egypt
and India. Ptolemy Philadelphus, who became king
in 285 B.C., founded Arsinoe near the head of the Red
Sea and completed or restored a canal connecting the
Red Sea with the Nile.[3] The chief port on the Red
Sea, however, was for some time Berenice, 500 miles
farther south, and goods were carried 200 miles overland from here to Coptos on the Nile. Later, Berenice
was superseded by Myoshormos, 250 miles farther
north. During the reign of the Ptolemies trade with
the Ethiopians, especially those at Meroe, was developed and the eastern tributary of the Nile, the
Astaboras, became known, and the Nile itself as far
as the junction with the Astapus (the Blue Nile).

[1] Mueller, *Frag. Hist. Graec.*, vol. ii; Strabo, ii, 1, 8–9.
[2] Strabo, xv, 1, 15.   [3] Herod., ii, 158.

XI. *The Discovery of Western Europe*

UNTIL about the beginning of the third century before Christ the history of the discovery of the world
is concerned chiefly with the coast of the Mediterranean Sea and the continent of Asia; in much less
degree with the continent of Africa. Though the
names of the Iberians, Celts, and certain peoples of
Italy were not unknown, the Greeks had little, if any,
definite knowledge of the interior of Spain or Gaul or
the peoples and places of central and northern Italy.
Of Germany and the western coast of Europe they
were absolutely ignorant. In view of the large Greek
population in Sicily and southern Italy, it is surprising that the Greeks appear to have taken so little
interest in the geography of this part of the world.
In fact it was not until Rome had established herself
as the military and commercial power of the central
and western Mediterranean that the discovery of a
large part of Europe began.

Though the date is doubtful, it was perhaps in the
latter part of the fourth century that Pytheas of
Massilia, one of the few real explorers of antiquity,
made a voyage to the north along the western coast
of Europe. He described the voyage and recorded
his observations in a book which soon disappeared
and which was discredited by some geographers, especially by Strabo, who often refers to Pytheas, but
takes every opportunity to brand him as a liar. From
quotations in Strabo [1] and Pliny [2] it appears that

[1] i, 4, 2–5; ii, 4, 1–2; ii, 5, 8; iv, 4, 1.
[2] *N. H.*, ii, 75 (187); iv, 16 (102); xxxvii, 2 (35–36).

Pytheas claimed to have sailed from Gades to the river Tanais. He mentioned the projection on the western coast of Gaul (Brittany) and a group of islands off the coast, which Strabo regards as a mere invention. Cantium (Kent) in Britain, he says, is a voyage of several days from Gaul. According to Polybius, quoted by Strabo, Pytheas claimed to have traveled over all Britain. Though he did not say that he had visited it, he brought back a report of an island called Thule, a voyage of six days north of Britain, where day and night lasted each six months. According to Pliny, Pytheas mentioned a people called Guiones or Gutones (the Goths), who lived on a gulf of the ocean. A day's sail from their country was an island, Abalus, where amber was gathered, which was sold to the neighboring Teutoni. Timaeus, Pliny says, accepted this statement of Pytheas, but called the island Basilia.

It is impossible to determine the extent of this exploration of Pytheas. He may have sailed all the way around Britain. He may even have entered the Baltic Sea and reached the river Vistula. It is more probable, however, that he sailed no farther than the Elbe, and, if his claim is correctly reported, that he mistook that river for the Tanais, though, if he knew his geography, he must have been surprised to find the river flowing north into the northern ocean.

Pytheas was apparently a good astronomer, for he fixed within a few miles the latitude of Massilia, a reckoning that was used by Ptolemy as a basis for his map of the western Mediterranean. He took obser-

vations for latitude also during his voyage. Even
Strabo accepts his calculations.

Several works written at the end of the fourth century or in the first half of the third showed an in-
creasing knowledge of the western countries. Timaeus
of Tauromenium wrote a history of Sicily [1] in which
he gave an account of the Etruscans, Romans, Ligurians, Celts, and Iberians, getting a good deal of his
information, it is said, from Pytheas. In his *History
of Plants*,[2] which is still in existence, Theophrastus
of Lesbos describes the trees and plants of Latium.
In the work *De Mirabilibus*, ascribed to Aristotle, but
really dating from the third century before Christ,
there are references to the iron mines of Elba, the
Hercynian Forest as the source of the Danube, and
the Rhine as a river flowing past the land of the Germans. This is the earliest reference to the Germans.
The author of this work says that on a voyage four
days west of the Pillars of Hercules the Phoenicians
found dry land at low tide. He speaks also of an
island with rivers and trees in the same part of the
ocean, — evidently one of the group called the Fortunate Islands (that is, the Canaries).

XII. *The Geographers of the Third and Second Centuries*

THE first serious attempts at mathematical geography, that is, the first efforts to determine precise location and distance by means of latitude and longitude,

[1] Mueller, *Frag. Hist. Graec.*, vol. I.   [2] v, 8, 3.

were made in the third century. Eratosthenes, who
was born at Cyrene and was librarian at Alexandria
from 240 to 196, has been called the father of scientific geography because he was chiefly interested in
these matters. His geography, of which only fragments [1] survive, was in three books. In the first he
discussed the form and nature of the earth and the
changes in its surface; the second was mathematical;
the third contained the description of countries, po-
litic?l conditions, etc. He estimated the circumference of the earth at about 29,000 miles,[2] but his attempts to discover the distance of the sun and moon
from the earth were not so successful. His calculations for the earth were based upon a main parallel
of latitude running from the Pillars of Hercules
through Rhodes, Issus, Thapsacus on the Euphrates,
the Caspian Gates, and the Indian Caucasus, to the
eastern ocean.[3] In Asia this line followed the Taurus
Mountains, conceived as a series of parallel ranges
running east and west and ending on the eastern
coast in an imaginary promontory called Tamarus.
The distances in Asia he got largely from the accounts
of the expedition of Alexander and the operations of
Seleucus. At a right angle to this parallel of latitude
was a meridian beginning at Meroe on the Nile and
passing through Syene, Alexandria, Rhodes, and
Byzantium, to the mouth of the Borysthenes.

It is interesting to note that Eratosthenes, the
scientist, unlike most of the ancient geographers, did

---

[1] H. Berger, *Die geographischen Fragmente des Eratosthenes.*
[2] Cleomedes, *The Circular Motion of the Heavenly Bodies,* i, 10.
[3] Strabo, ii, 1, 1.

not credit Homer with any knowledge of remote places.[1] On the other hand, he accepted Pytheas for western Europe and even admitted the existence of Thule.[2] He probably had no knowledge of the country north of the Alps and the Danube and regarded the Caspian Sea as an inlet from the northern ocean. He undoubtedly assumed that the eastern ocean was directly east of India and that the Ganges flowed into it. He placed Taprobane (Ceylon) a voyage of seven days from the mainland.[3] About Arabia he knew more than any earlier writer.

In mathematical geography Eratosthenes was followed by Hipparchus,[4] an astronomer of Nicaea in Bithynia, whose only extant work is his commentary on Aratus. He conceived the idea of a complete map of the earth based upon a system of parallels and meridians. Strabo [5] gives ten of his parallels. The southernmost passed through the so-called Cinnamon Country (the projection on the eastern coast of Africa south of Arabia) and Taprobane; the northernmost given by Strabo was just north of the Maeotis. There were many inaccuracies, as was inevitable on account of the lack of proper instruments for determining location.

A geographer of a quite different sort was the historian Polybius from Megalopolis in Arcadia, who lived in Rome as a hostage for seventeen years after the defeat of Perseus in 167 B.C. He traveled in Gaul,

[1] Strabo, i, 2, 7, 15.   [2] *Ibid.*, 4, 3.   [3] *Ibid.*, xv, 1, 14.
[4] H. Berger, *Die geographischen Fragmente des Hipparchus*; Strabo, i, 1, 12.
[5] ii, 5, 34–42.

Spain, and Africa, was present at the destruction of Carthage in 146, and was probably at Numantia in 134.[1] There were forty books in his history, but only the first five and fragments of others survive. The thirty-fourth book was on the subject of geography, and most of the extant fragments are passages quoted by Strabo. In his attitude toward geography, in his realization of the importance of geography as an aid to history, Polybius resembles Herodotus, though it has been said that, on account of his lack of imagination, he fails to visualize the places that he describes and, therefore, is not clear. However that may be, he shows better than any other the state of geographical knowledge in the second century before Christ, a state due in large part to the gradual accumulation of information rather than to specific explorations or conquests.

Polybius regarded the Tanais as the boundary between Europe and Asia, and the Nile as the boundary between Asia and Africa.[2] He rejected the story of Pytheas [3] and, therefore, had little to say about the Atlantic coast of Europe. His knowledge of Spain was far greater than that of any earlier writer; [4] he mentions several rivers, the Pyrenees Mountains, and many tribes and cities. He knew less about Gaul, but locates the mouth of the Liger [5] (Loire) and says that the Morini are separated from Britain by a narrow strait.[6] He was well informed about the Alps, though he assumed that the whole system extended east and

---

[1] Polybius, iii, 59; Cicero, *ad Fam.*, v, 13, 2.   [2] iii, 37 ff.
[3] *Ibid.*, 38; xxxiv, 5.   [4] xxxiv, 8–10.   [5] *Ibid.*, 10.
[6] Pliny, *N. H.*, iv, 23 (122).

west, and speaks of four passes, one of them being
the route taken by Hannibal, which Polybius says
that he himself had visited.[1] He describes correctly
the lakes of northern Italy.[2] As a result of his long
residence in Rome he undoubtedly knew Italy much
better than any of his predecessors. He had correct
information about the eastern coast of the Adriatic,
and no doubt profited by the fact that the Romans
had built a military road, the *Via Egnatia*, from
Apollonia to Thessalonica,[3] and by measuring the
miles and placing milestones had established accurate
distances for this region. He was well informed about
the Euxine and the Maeotis and knew that the latter
was not nearly so large as his predecessors had
thought.[4] Regarding Asia he knew no more than earlier writers, but he was better informed about the
northern coast of Africa. Pliny says [5] that after the
Third Punic War Scipio gave to Polybius ships for
the exploration of the western coast of Africa, but
there is no other reference to it.

During the second century and the early part of the
first there were several other writers on geographical
subjects, whose works are not extant. One of the
more important was Agatharchides [6] of Cnidus, who
was tutor of Ptolemy Soter II. He wrote a work on
Asia, another on Europe, and one in five books on the
Erythraean Sea and the peoples about it; of the last
Photius has preserved extracts from the first and fifth
books. There is a good description of both coasts of

[1] iii, 48.   [2] Strabo, iv, 6, 12.
[3] *Ibid.*, vii, 7, 4.   [4] iv, 39.   [5] *N. H.*, v, 1 (9).
[6] Mueller, *Geog. Graec. Min.*, vol. i.

the Red Sea and an account of the Arabian tribes, especially the Sabaei, who lived in Arabia Felix, a region of great wealth, which carried on trade with India and had a caravan route to Petra, the capital of Arabia Petraea in the northwestern part of the country. Agatharchides was the chief source of information about the Ethiopians for Strabo and Pliny.

Another geographer of this period was Artemidorus [1] of Ephesus, a student and traveler, who wrote a general treatise, which included a *periplus* of the Mediterranean Sea and one of the Red Sea. He appears to have been more accurate than his predecessors in the matter of distances and was the first to give the course of the Ganges correctly.[2] He was one of Strabo's chief authorities.

Posidonius, who was the head of the Stoic school at Rhodes and the teacher of Cicero, was a great traveler and a prolific writer on many subjects, including geography.[3] Strabo [4] quotes from him an interesting story about a voyage made by a man named Eudoxus, from Cyzicus, who was sent on a mission to Alexandria. While he was there, an Indian whose vessel had been wrecked in the Red Sea was brought to the king, and offered, if the king would provide a ship, to take it to India. The arrangement was made and Eudoxus went on the ship. If the story is true, this was the earliest voyage directly from Egypt to India. The vessel returned with spices and

---

[1] R. Stiehle, *Der Geograph Artemidorus von Ephesos, Philologus*, vol. XI (1856).

[2] Strabo, xv, 1, 72.

[3] Mueller, *Frag. Hist. Graec.*, vol. III.   [4] ii, 3, 4.

precious stones and, the king having died, his wife sent Eudoxus on a second voyage, which also was successful. On the return, however, the ship was driven out of its course, and brought back from the African coast south of Ethiopia the curved prow of a boat, which was believed to have come from the West and was recognized as like those of Gades. This inspired Eudoxus to undertake the circumnavigation of Africa. He got a ship from Cyzicus, and, with two lighter ones, started from Gades. The larger vessel was wrecked and another had to be built. The expedition finally reached a tribe of Ethiopians who spoke the same language as those on the eastern coast. Here Eudoxus turned back and, after an unsuccessful attempt to induce the king of Mauretania to fit out a new expedition, returned to Gades. At a later time he is said to have made a second start, but the story of Posidonius breaks off at this point.

XIII. *Roman Military Operations*

DURING the period from the middle of the second century before Christ to the end of the reign of Augustus the Romans contributed largely to geographical knowledge by military operations in Europe and, in less degree, in Asia and Africa. No part of the Roman domain in Europe was a source of so much trouble as Spain. Though it was organized into two provinces in 197 and Roman colonies were founded, there were frequent revolts, which culminated in the war with Numantia, lasting from 143 to 133. Even after that and until the time of Augustus there were

insurrections that demanded the constant presence
of Roman troops. On the coast of Gaul the tribes on
either side of the Rhone were subjugated in 121, and
a few years later the colony of Narbo was founded.
The Dalmatians on the eastern coast of the Adriatic
were reduced in 119. C. Scribonius Curio, who was
governor of Macedonia in 75, reached the Danube
in the course of a war with the Moesians and Dar-
danians.

The operations of Caesar in Gaul and Britain were
geographically of great importance. In 58 in the campaign against Ariovistus he led a Roman army to the
Rhine. In the war with the Belgae in 57 a legion was
sent to the Atlantic coast. In 56 in the war with the
Veneti, Caesar fought against forces from Britain. In
55 he crossed the Rhine into Germany on a bridge
probably between the modern Coblenz and Ander-
nach. In the same year, with two legions, he went to
Britain, crossing from a place called Portus Itius
(probably Boulogne or Wissant) and landing near
Deal, a few miles north of Dover. This he regarded
as only a preliminary expedition. In the following
year, with a large fleet, five legions, and 2,000 cavalry,
he crossed again from Gaul, fought a battle twelve
miles from the coast, and crossed the Thames. He
took the town of Cassivelaunus and the Britons sur-
rendered. During the following years he was occupied with insurrections in Gaul, but in 53 he again
crossed the Rhine to attack the Suevi. In this connection he describes in his *Commentaries* [1] the Her-

[1] *B. G.*, vi, 24–25,

cynian Forest, though the passage has been criticized as an interpolation.

Caesar must be credited with the dissemination of much new information regarding Gaul and Britain. In his *Commentaries* [1] he describes Britain as follows:

A triangular island with one side, about 500 miles long, opposite Gaul; one end of this side, the one in Kent, faces east, the other faces south. The second side, 700 miles long, faces Spain and the west; on this side is Hibernia (Ireland), half as large as Britain, and between them is Mona (the Isle of Man, elsewhere called Monapia); there are thought to be several other islands where, according to some writers, at the time of the winter solstice, night lasts for thirty days. The third side of Britain, 800 miles long, faces north and there is no land opposite; one end of this side is toward Germany.

The dimensions given in this passage are a great improvement on those ascribed to Pytheas, but the incorrect orientation gave authority to a misconception that persisted for a long time.

Though the chief interest of Augustus was in the organization of the empire rather than in the extension of its territory, there were in his reign some military operations that contributed to geographical knowledge. In northern Spain the Cantabri and Asturi were subdued in 22. In central Europe, Raetia, Noricum, Pannonia, and Moesia were organized as provinces, and the Danube thus became throughout its course the northern boundary of the empire. In Germany, Drusus, a step-son of Augustus, crossed the Rhine in 12 B.C. and, after a campaign against the Usipetes and Sigambri, sailed along the coast of Germany to the river Amisia (the Ems), the first Roman

[1] *B. G.*, v, 13,

to navigate the northern ocean. Entering Germany
again in 11 B.C., Drusus advanced as far as the Visur-
gis (the Weser), and in a third invasion in 9 B.C. he
reached the Albis (the Elbe), about 300 miles from
the Rhine. In A.D. 4 and again in A.D. 5 Tiberius,
who had succeeded his brother Drusus, advanced as
far as the Albis. In the course of the latter campaign,
the Roman fleet sailed to the mouth of the river and
went up to join the land-forces. Besides a greatly increased knowledge of this part of Germany, the Romans probably got information about the peninsula
of Jutland and a bay farther east called Codanus
Sinus, that is, the Baltic Sea.

Regarding Asia, in spite of Roman occupation and
the organization of provinces, it can hardly be said
that the Romans added much to geographical knowledge during this period. Lucullus was the first Roman general to lead an army to the Euphrates and
Tigris, but this part of Asia was already well known.
This was in 69 B.C. Pompey succeeded Lucullus in 66
and, after defeating Mithridates and Tigranes, subdued the Iberians and Albanians, who lived between
the Euxine and the Caspian, incidentally contributing to the knowledge of this little-known region. In
34 an expedition under Antony went through Armenia into Atropatene, southwest of the Caspian,
the most distant point in that direction ever reached
by a Roman army. Strabo [1] has preserved an account of the expedition of Aelius Gallus into Arabia
in 24. With a thousand men he went down the Red

[1] xvi, 4, 22–24.

Sea to Leuce Come in Arabia. From here he marched
for many days into the interior and is said to have
taken many cities, but it is impossible to identify
them. Lack of water forced him to return. It may be
noted that during this period the name of the Seres,
the silk-producing people of the Far East, was becoming known to the Romans. With the exception of a
statement in Strabo [1] to the effect that the Bactrian
kings extended their power as far as the Seres, the
earliest reference to them is in the *Georgics* of Vergil.[2]

In Africa the war with Jugurtha added little to
geographical knowledge, though a Roman army went
as far south as Capsa and the river Muluccha, the
boundary between Numidia and Mauretania.[3] In
connection with the history of this war there are
allusions to an island or islands outside the Pillars
of Hercules, undoubtedly the Canary or, possibly,
Madeira Islands. Diodorus [4] tells of a Carthaginian
vessel that was blown out to sea and several days'
sail from the mainland came upon a large island.
Eudoxus, too, was said to have found here an uninhabited island, and Plutarch [5] tells how in Sulla's
time Sertorius had met sailors in Spain who had just
come from the Atlantic Islands, 10,000 stadia from
the coast of Africa. These were probably the Madeira
Islands. In 22 Petronius, governor of Egypt, led an
expedition into Ethiopia against Queen Candace,
taking several towns and advancing as far as Napata,
not far north of Meroe.[6] In 20 Cornelius Balbus, gov-

[1] xi, 11, 1.   [2] ii, 121.   [3] Sall., *Jug.*, 89–92, 110.
[4] v, 19–20.   [5] Sertorius, 8.   [6] Strabo, xvii, 1, 54.

ernor of Africa, marched against the Garamantes and reached Phazania on the northern edge of the desert south of the Lesser Syrtis.[1]

XIV. *Geographical Works of the First Century B.C.*

DURING this period of military activity there were in the field of literature very few contributions to geography, — no others so important as Caesar's account of his campaigns in Gaul and Britain, which has already been mentioned. Diodorus the Sicilian wrote a history of the world in forty books, of which fifteen survive. These contain some valuable geographical material, — a treatment of the Ethiopian peoples on the Red Sea [2] and descriptions of the British Islands [3] and the Balearic Islands.[4] Diodorus is the first to give names to all three corners of Britain, — Cantium, Bolerium (Land's End), and Horcas.[5] He gives also an interesting account [6] of the exportation of tin from Cornwall; in his time it was shipped from the island of Ictis (Saint Michaels Mount near Land's End) to Gaul, where it was carried overland in thirty days to the mouth of the Rhone.

The younger Juba, King of Numidia (later King of Mauretania), was a very learned man, educated at Rome, and was the author of many works on various subjects, of which only fragments remain.[7] He wrote

[1] Pliny, *N. H.*, v, 5 (36).   [2] iii, 11.   [3] v, 21–22.
[4] *Ibid.*, 17.   [5] *Ibid.*, 21.   [6] *Ibid.*, 22.
[7] Mueller, *Frag. Hist. Graec.*, vol. III.

descriptions of Africa and Arabia,[1] and made a special study of the Fortunate Islands [2] (the Canaries). He had an elaborate theory regarding the source of the Nile,[3] placing it in the mountains of western Mauretania, a theory reminiscent of that of Herodotus.

Other writings of less importance may be briefly mentioned. Sallust, the first governor of Numidia, in his *War with Jugurtha*, gives information that he had gathered about the surrounding country. Statius Sebosus wrote a book about the western coast of Africa and the islands west of Africa.[4] Isidorus of Charax in Babylonia wrote a general work on geography; the brief extant guide-book for Parthia [5] is probably a part of that work. Varro Atacinus wrote a geographical poem.[6] Pomponius Mela [7] and Pliny [8] quote from Nepos an incredible story that certain Indians who had been brought as a gift to Metellus Celer, governor of Gaul, had been carried around by storms north of Asia and Europe and had landed on the coast of Germany.

In this connection may be mentioned a map of the world, prepared by order of Agrippa, which was painted on a wall of the *Porticus Vipsania* in Rome and was probably reproduced in various parts of the empire. A commentary on this was issued, giving distances and the length and breadth of the provinces.[9] Some of the information was apparently

---

[1] Pliny, *N. H.*, xii, 31 (56).   [2] *Ibid.*, vi, 32 (203).
[3] *Ibid.*, v, 9 (51–53).   [4] *Ibid.*, vi, 31–32 (201–202).
[5] Mueller, *Geog. Graec. Min.*, vol. I.
[6] Pliny, *N. H.*, i, in his catalogue of authorities.
[7] iii, 5, 45.   [8] *N. H.*, ii, 67 (170).   [9] Pliny, *N. H.*, iii, 2 (17).

based upon insufficient evidence, as, for example, the statement that the mouth of the Danube was a thousand Roman miles from the northern ocean.[1] Within the boundaries of the empire, however, distances were no doubt based upon the itineraries of Roman roads which were now being published and were of great geographical value. These early itineraries have disappeared. Those still existing date from the fourth century.

XV. *Strabo*

THE most important geographical work of antiquity is that of Strabo, a native of Amasia in Pontus. He was born probably in 64 or 63 B.C., lived for several years in Rome, and spent much time also at Alexandria. Like Herodotus and Polybius he was a great traveler. He himself tells us [2] that he has journeyed toward the west from Armenia to Tyrrhenia and toward the south from the Euxine to the borders of Ethiopia. He lived until A.D. 21. Besides his geographical work he wrote a voluminous work on general history, probably covering the period from 146 to 31 B.C. This is not extant.

Strabo was already an elderly man when he began his geography and it is commonly believed that he died before it was finished. There should be noted, however, a recent theory that the work was first published about 7 B.C., but appeared in a revised edition about A.D. 18, with numerous insertions, chiefly complimentary to the emperor Tiberius. There were

Pliny, *N. H.*, iv, 12 (81).   [2] ii, 5, 11.

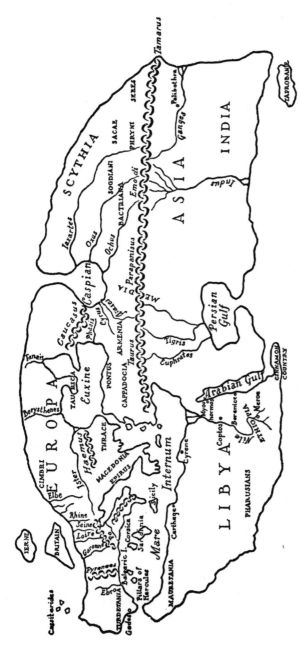

THE WORLD ACCORDING TO STRABO

seventeen books and these have all come down to us, with the exception of the latter part of the seventh, of which there is only a summary. The treatment is historical, political, and mythological, as well as physical, and is intended for the general reader of intelligence. Strabo was not a scientist, nor was he as scholarly as Herodotus, whose work he treats with contempt. He had the wisdom, however, to recognize certain limitations. He mentions the difficulty of transferring lines and places from a curved surface to a flat one, but consoles himself with the statement that it makes little difference.[1] It must be admitted in his defence that there could be little advance in scientific geography without observations that would determine latitude and longitude. With due allowance for this limitation, however, it may be said that he accepts many things which are not proved or are even obviously impossible. Homer he seems to regard as the source of all knowledge. The voyage of the Argonauts is to him a real voyage and, in general, he treats mythology as seriously as if it were history. He rejects absolutely the discoveries of Pytheas and does not avail himself of recent geographical sources, as, for example, Sallust and Juba. On the other hand, he makes use of Caesar's *Commentaries* and quotes largely from earlier writers whose works are no longer in existence. In fact we are greatly indebted to him for much of our knowledge of these earlier geographers. On the whole, in spite of the lack of scientific treatment and in spite of errors, many of which

[1] ii, 5, 10.

might easily have been avoided, Strabo's work is exceedingly valuable, as indicating the progress of geographical study and the knowledge of the world at the beginning of the Christian era.

The first two books form a general but very unsystematic introduction. After a long discussion of Homeric geography the author considers the work of Eratosthenes, Posidonius, Polybius, and other earlier geographers and incidentally gives at considerable length his own views on the general aspects of the subject. He believes the earth to be a sphere in the centre of the universe. The greatest length of the habitable part of the earth is 70,000 stadia (about 8,000 miles), the greatest width 30,000 stadia (about 3,400 miles).[1] The northern limit of this habitable belt is about 460 miles north of the mouth of the river Borysthenes, on a parallel extending north of Ireland, which Strabo, disbelieving the existence of Thule, places north of Britain and regards as the northernmost point in the habitable world.[2] The southern limit is about 350 miles south of Meroe, just south of the Cinnamon country and Taprobane.[3] The interesting suggestion is made [4] that there may be one or more other inhabited worlds in the north temperate zone, an idea that Seneca may have had in mind in a well-known passage of the *Medea*.[5] The habitable world, that is, Europe, Asia, and Africa, as known at the time, is surrounded by the ocean. The Caspian, Persian, Arabian, and Mediterranean Seas are inlets from this surrounding ocean.[6]

[1] ii, 5, 6.   [2] *Ibid.*, 5, 8–9.   [3] *Ibid.*, 5, 7.
[4] i, 4, 6; ii, 5, 13.   [5] 376–380.   [6] ii, 5, 18.

Strabo gives eight books to Europe, six to Asia, and one to Africa. His conception of Europe is badly distorted. He thinks that a line drawn from the Pillars of Hercules to the Strait of Messina runs through the middle of the Mediterranean, equidistant from Europe and Africa.[1] The Bay of Biscay faces north and the mouths of the Garonne, Loire, and Seine are all opposite Britain.[2] The mouth of the Rhine is on the same parallel as that of the Danube, and the mouth of the Borysthenes on the same parallel as northern Britain.[3] Though he describes the Apennines as extending from north to south,[4] his conception of the western Mediterranean forced him to give to the peninsula an exaggerated trend to the east.

The detailed description of the various parts of the world begins with Spain in the third book. The author was familiar with its chief geographical features, though he did not use Roman sources of information, but depended chiefly upon Artemidorus, Polybius, and Posidonius. The river Ebro, he says,[5] flows toward the south and is parallel with the Pyrenees. He gives [6] a detailed account of Gades and speaks [7] with admiration of Turdetania, formerly Tartessus. He describes [8] the Balearic Islands and says [9] that the Cassiterides (the Tin Islands) are far out at sea, north of the northwest corner of Spain and in about the same latitude as Britain.

In the fourth book the author discusses the geography of Gaul, Britain, Ireland, and the Alps. In

---

[1] ii, 5, 8.
[2] Ibid., 5, 28; iv, 5, 2.
[3] ii, 5, 8.
[4] Ibid., 5, 28.
[5] iii, 4, 6.
[6] Ibid., 5, 3–10.
[7] Ibid., 2, 14–15.
[8] Ibid., 5, 1–2.
[9] ii, 5, 15.

spite of incorrect orientation he is well acquainted with the physical features and peoples of Gaul. He gives [1] a minute and accurate description of Gallia Narbonensis and shows a superficial knowledge of the more remote parts, taken mainly from Caesar. Agrippa had recently built four main roads radiating from Lyons, but Strabo makes no use of the itineraries for Gaul. Of Britain he knows only what he got from Caesar, but, unlike Caesar, he puts the longest side opposite Gaul. Kent, he says, is opposite the mouth of the Rhine, and the southwest corner of the island is opposite the Pyrenees.[2] Ireland, as already stated, is north of Britain.[3] For the Alps Polybius is his chief authority, but he knows more than Polybius about their general configuration and the rivers flowing from them.[4] He gives an interesting account of the people living there, and speaks of carriage-roads across Mount Genèvre and the Little St. Bernard.[5]

The fifth and sixth books contain a description of Italy and the neighboring islands, which is in the main correct, in spite of the author's peculiar orientation of Italy. The Po, he says,[6] is the largest river in Europe except the Danube. He rejects the identification of the Po with the Eridanus and says that there is no river Eridanus.[7] He was apparently much interested in volcanoes. He says [8] that Vesuvius had been active, but, on account of lack of fuel, had become idle, and he describes [9] the eruptions of Aetna, which was visited by travelers in his time. He men-

---

[1] iv, 1, 3 ff.   [2] i, 4, 3; iv, 5, 1.   [3] ii, 5, 8.
[4] v, 1, 3.   [5] iv, 1, 3; 6, 1–12.   [6] *Ibid.*, 6, 5.
[7] v, 1, 9.   [8] *Ibid.*, 4, 8.   [9] vi, 2, 3, and 8.

tions also the volcanoes of the Aeolian Islands and
says that a small island had recently appeared on the
surface of the sea off the coast of Sicily.[1] Speaking of
Brundisium, he takes occasion to describe the Via
Appia.[2] The sixth book ends with a sketch of the
extent and condition of the Roman Empire.

There follows in the seventh book an account of the
countries east of the Rhine and west of the Tanais,
including Epirus, Macedonia, and Thrace. This book
is incomplete, the part relating to Macedonia and
Thrace having disappeared; there are, however, epit-
omes of the missing portion. The author was familiar with the discoveries of the Romans in western
Germany and mentions the rivers between the Rhine
and the Elbe and the tribes of that region.[3] He discusses [4] the Cimbri, but does not know the Cimbric
Chersonesus, and has no knowledge of the Baltic Sea
or the tradition of a large island there (probably
Scandinavia). In fact he says [5] that everything beyond the Elbe is unknown. He has correct information about Mount Haemus [6] (the Balkans) and the
Tauric Chersonesus,[7] but knows little about the country north and northwest of the Euxine, partly because
he did not accept the statements of Herodotus.

The eighth, ninth, and tenth books contain a long
and unsatisfactory description of Greece, founded
largely upon Homer and overloaded with literary
and mythological digressions. As in the case of Italy,
Greece is curiously distorted. Corinth is regarded as

---

[1] vi, 2, 11.   [2] *Ibid.*, 3, 7.   [3] vii, 1, 3-4.   [4] *Ibid.*, 2, 1-3.
[5] *Ibid.*, 2, 4.   [6] *Ibid.*, 5, 1.   [7] *Ibid.*, 4, 5.

the most eastern part of the Peloponnesus [1] and
Sunium is only a little farther north than Malea.[2]

In his description of Asia Strabo follows Eratosthenes in the idea that the continent is divided by
mountain-ranges extending all the way across from
west to east.[3] These are known as Taurus in the
west, as Parapanisus in central Asia, and then continue under various names to the eastern ocean,
where they end in the promontory of Tamarus.[4] In
the eleventh book there is an account, first, of the
country and peoples between the Tanais and the
Caspian; secondly, those east of the Caspian, as far
as the Scythians north of India; thirdly, those
bounded by the Caucasus Mountains and the Caspian on the north and by the Taurus Mountains on
the south. Regarding the length of the Maeotis from
north to south Strabo is more nearly correct than any
other ancient geographer.[5] The Caucasus Mountains
he describes [6] accurately and in detail, but underestimates their length; that is, he makes what he calls the
isthmus between the Euxine and the Caspian too
narrow. He describes [7] the city of Dioscurias at the
eastern end of the Euxine, a great commercial centre
which carried on trade with the east through the
rivers Phasis and Cyrus. In Strabo's time the Cyrus
and the Araxes appear to have entered the Caspian
by separate mouths.[8] The Caspian is regarded [9] as
an inlet from the northern ocean and its dimension

---

[1] viii, 2, 1.   [2] ii, 1, 40.   [3] Ibid., 5, 31.
[4] xi, 11, 7.   [5] Ibid., 2, 3.   [6] Ibid., 2, 15.
[7] Ibid., 2, 16.   [8] Ibid., 4, 2.   [9] Ibid., 6, 1.

from east to west is about the same as that from
north to south. The river Iaxartes flows into the
Caspian and is the boundary between the Sacae and
the Sogdiani.[1] On the authority of Apollodorus of
Artemita, Strabo says [2] that the empire of the Bactrian kings extended at one time as far as the Seres
and the Phryni. Returning to the west he describes
Armenia and Media and the courses of the Euphrates
and Tigris. In his account of Armenia he is far in advance of Eratosthenes, since this part of Asia had
become known through the campaigns of Lucullus
and Pompey in the Mithridatic wars.

In the twelfth, thirteenth, and fourteenth books
there is an account of Asia Minor, including Cappa-
docia and Pontus. The description of Pontus is excellent, and that of the western coast and the adja-
cent islands is perhaps the best part of the whole
work. The treatment of the interior is somewhat
meagre.

The fifteenth and sixteenth books are given to the
southern part of the continent. The treatment of
India is interesting, but shows no advance in geographical knowledge, being taken largely from Megasthenes or from earlier writers who had accompanied
Alexander. The Ganges, generally regarded as the
largest river in the world, flows from the Emodi
Mountains (the Himalayas) first south and then east
to Palibothra and the eastern ocean.[3] The greatest
length of India is east and west. Strabo, like Eratosthenes, had an exaggerated idea of the size of the

[1] ii, 7, 4.   [2] *Ibid.*, 11, 1.   [3] xv, 1, 72.

Persian Gulf, believing it to be nearly as large as the
Euxine.[1] For the interior of Arabia he uses the story
of the expedition of Aelius Gallus.

In the last book, the seventeenth, the author gives
a brief account of Africa, treating Egypt, however,
especially the Nile, in considerable detail. The continent, he says,[2] is shaped like a right-angled triangle;
the northern coast from the Nile to the Pillars of
Hercules is the base, and at a right-angle to this is the
side formed by the Nile, continued to the southern
ocean; the hypothenuse is the southern coast from
Ethiopia to Mauretania. He speaks[3] of the canal
from the head of the Red Sea to the eastern arm of the
Nile and mentions[4] the caravan route from Coptos
to Berenice, though the latter had by this time been
superseded by Myoshormos. He gives a full and
correct account of the northern coast from Carthage
to Cyrene and is the first writer to give definite information about the oases of the desert. He even mentions[5] the Pharusians and other peoples who lived
south of the desert. He apparently has no knowledge
of the western coast.

XVI. *Pomponius Mela*

GEOGRAPHY as an independent subject is almost com-
pletely lacking in the history of Latin literature.
Historians introduced geographical material incidentally as a mere background. A few writers described their own travels and what they themselves

---

[1] xvi, 3, 2.   [2] xvii, 3, 1.   [3] *Ibid.*, 1, 26.
[4] *Ibid.*, 1, 45.   [5] *Ibid.*, 3, 7.

had seen. In the encyclopedic work of the older Pliny
four books of the thirty-seven are given to a comprehensive treatment of geography. But the only Latin
work of the classical period which is exclusively geographical is the *De Chorographia* of Pomponius Mela.

Mela was a native of Tingentera in southern Spain.
His work was written after A.D. 43, since he speaks [1]
of an expedition to Britain which was probably the
one made by the emperor Claudius in that year. It
has been claimed that the passage in question refers
to an expedition begun by Caligula, and that, therefore, the work was composed in 40 or 41, but the argument is not convincing. Mela was not a scholar and
his work is neither scientific nor even accurate. As a
matter of fact it was not intended to be scholarly. In
his preface the author disclaims any ambition of that
sort, promises to be brief, and says that he will con-
fine his attention to things that are most clear. It
was evidently his intention to make his work as interesting as possible, and he does succeed in relieving
the dryness of the subject, especially by the insertion
of fables told by Herodotus and others. In spite of
the unscholarly nature of the treatment, however,
the work is valuable as showing the geographical
conceptions of the average citizen of the time. Moreover, it is possible at certain points to discover an advance in geographical knowledge beyond the limits
of Strabo, whose work had appeared not many years
before.

The three books of Mela contain a description of

[1] iii, 49.

the coast of the Mediterranean Sea and the coast of
the ocean surrounding the earth. The plan of the
work and its comparative brevity made it impossible
for the author to say very much about the interior.
At the beginning of the first book there are a few
chapters of a general nature containing a discussion
of the shape of the earth, the zones, continents, etc.
The Tanais is the boundary between Europe and
Asia, the Nile the boundary between Asia and Africa.[1]
All around is the ocean, from which there are four inlets, — the Caspian, Persian, Arabian, and Mediterranean Seas,[2] the last being called "our sea" (*mediter-
raneum* as an adjective was first used by Solinus [3] in
the third century and, as a proper name, by Isidorus [4]
in the seventh century). In the far south beyond the
ocean is the land of the Antichthones.[5]

After these preliminary chapters the author starts
from the Pillars of Hercules and follows the southern
and eastern coasts of the Mediterranean to the
Euxine and then the coast of the Euxine and Maeotis
to the mouth of the river Tanais. In the second book
he continues his course around the Euxine to Thrace
and then follows the coasts of Greece, Italy, Gaul,
and Spain to the Pillars of Hercules. At the end of
this book he describes the islands of the Mediterranean. The first two books naturally offer little of
geographical interest, as they treat regions that were
by this time more or less familiar to everyone.

In the third book, which in many ways is far more

[1] i, 8.   [2] *Ibid.*, 5–6.   [3] 18, 23.
[4] *Etymolog.*, xiii, 16.   [5] Pomp. Mela, i, 4.

interesting, Mela starts again from the Pillars of Hercules and traces the coast of the encircling ocean around Europe, Asia, and Africa, returning to his starting-point. In the middle of this book he describes the islands off the coast of Spain and those in the northern ocean, including Britain. He is well informed regarding the western coast of Spain and Gaul, though he makes the common error of believing that the coast of Gaul extended from the Pyrenees toward the east or northeast.[1] That is, he has no proper knowledge of the Bay of Biscay and does not realize that this part of the coast of Gaul runs north and south, though he describes [2] the mouth of the Garonne in picturesque detail and speaks [3] of the projection on the western coast of Gaul. He says [4] that Britain is triangular, with a wide angle facing the mouth of the Rhine; one side faces Gaul, another Germany. Beyond Britain is Iuverna (Ireland), which is nearly as large as Britain.[5] He is the first writer who mentions the Orcades, and he mentions also the Shetland Islands, calling them the Haemodae.[6]

Mela shows a definite advance beyond Strabo in his knowledge of the northern coast of Germany. Beyond the Elbe, he says,[7] is a large bay called Codanus, containing many islands, the largest being Codannovia. This is undoubtedly a reference to the Baltic Sea and Scandinavia. He speaks [8] of the river Vistula as the boundary between the Hermiones and

[1] iii, 12.
[2] *Ibid.*, 21–22.
[3] *Ibid.*, 16.
[4] *Ibid.*, 50.
[5] *Ibid.*, 53.
[6] *Ibid.*, 54.
[7] *Ibid.*, 31 and 54.
[8] *Ibid.*, 33.

the Sarmatians. He still has the notion of the old
Greek geographers that a branch of the Danube
flowed into the Adriatic.[1] He believes in the existence
of the Rhipaean Mountains in the far north and
thinks that the Hyperboreans live still farther north
in a region where day and night continue each for six
months.[2] The Caspian Sea, he thinks,[3] is connected
with the northern ocean by a long narrow strait like
a river, a conception due, perhaps, to vague rumors
of the river Volga.

His description of the eastern coast of Asia is, naturally, very meagre. From the northeastern corner of
Asia, which he calls the Scythian Promontory, he says
that the coast extends south to a mountain called
Tabis, and then farther south to the promontory of
Tamos at the eastern extremity of the Taurus Mountains.[4] The Seres live between Tabis and Tamos,[5]
that is, north of Taurus. Near the promontory of
Tamos is an island called Chryse and at the mouth of
the Ganges, which flows into the eastern ocean still
farther south, is an island called Argyre.[6] It may be
no more than a coincidence that a hundred years later
Ptolemy calls the Malay Peninsula, east of India, the
Golden Peninsula, and gives the name Argyre to the
region on the east side of the Gulf of the Ganges,
but it is possible that even as early as Mela some
vague reports of lands east of India had reached the
western world. The southeastern corner of India and
of the Asiatic continent is a promontory called Colis.[7]

[1] ii, 57.   [2] iii, 36–37.   [3] *Ibid.*, 38.   [4] *Ibid.*, 59–68.
[5] i, 11; iii, 60.   [6] iii, 68–70.   [7] *Ibid.*, 68.

Regarding Taprobane (Ceylon) Mela is inclined to follow Hipparchus in the idea that it is the beginning of the land of the Antichthones in the southern hemisphere.[1]

In his treatment of Africa Mela seems to know that the eastern coast extends at least some distance south of the entrance to the Arabian Gulf.[2] Moreover, he is the first to bring out the fact that the western coast extends south (it really extends southwest) and not southeast from the Pillars of Hercules.[3] His brief description of the western coast makes it probable that he had seen the narrative of Hanno.[4] About the Nile he was apparently unable to decide whether it rose in the far west or in the land of the Antichthones, whence it flowed north under the sea, reappearing in Ethiopia.[5]

XVII. *Military Operations and Explorations in the First and Second Centuries A.D.*

AUGUSTUS had no ambition to increase the territory of the empire. It was his policy not to extend the frontiers beyond the Rhine, Danube, and Euphrates, and, in the main, this policy was observed until the reign of Trajan. In the first century the only increase in geographical knowledge through military operations was in Britain. The two expeditions of Julius Caesar had as their chief result the dissemination of definite information about the island, which hitherto

[1] iii, 70. [2] *Ibid.*, 89. [3] *Ibid.*, 100.
[4] *Ibid.*, 90 and 93. [5] i, 54; iii, 96.

had been only vaguely known through traders. The period of Roman conquest in Britain began in A.D. 43, when Aulus Plautius was sent there with four legions. The emperor himself accompanied the expedition, though he remained for only a short time. In 47 Ostorius Scapula succeeded Plautius and the whole southern part of the island including southern Wales was soon secured for Rome. In 61 Suetonius Paulinus took the island of Mona (Anglesey) off the northwestern corner of Wales. In the reign of Vespasian, Petilius Cerealis extended the Roman domain into what is now Yorkshire, the country of the Brigantes. Agricola was appointed governor in 78, subdued the Ordovices in northern Wales, and secured all the region south of the Forth and the Clyde. During these campaigns of Agricola an Irish chieftain, who had been expelled from Ireland, found refuge with the Roman army and from him the Romans got their first definite information about Ireland.

Prior to this time there had been little, if any, knowledge of Britain beyond the Forth and the Clyde, though the older Pliny mentions [1] the Caledonian Forest as the limit of Roman conquest and both Mela [2] and Pliny [3] have some information about the Orcades (the Orkneys) north of Britain. In 84, however, Agricola defeated the Caledonians, while the fleet sailed to the north along the eastern coast and subdued the Orcades. Land (the Shetland Islands) was seen still farther north, to which the sailors gave the name that Pytheas had used centuries before —

[1] N. H., iv, 30 (102).   [2] iii, 54.   [3] N. H., iv, 30 (103).

Thule. Tacitus speaks [1] of the red hair and large limbs of the Caledonians as indicating their German origin, while the Silures in southern Wales, he says, have dark curly hair because they live opposite Spain and are descended from Spanish colonists. Ireland, he says,[2] is midway between Britain and Spain.

This was the end of Rome's career of conquest in Britain. Through colonization and trade the geography of the island came to be a matter of common knowledge, though the northern and western parts were never thoroughly subdued, and Britain was never Romanized to the same extent as Gaul. In the second century two walls were built as a defence against the northern tribes, — one by Hadrian between the Tyne and the Solway, the other by Antoninus Pius between the Forth and the Clyde.

The Rhine had been definitely accepted as the boundary between Germany and the empire, and such knowledge of Germany as the Romans had at this time must have come largely from traders and from the peoples living along the Rhine. Only in southwestern Germany did the Romans secure a permanent foothold. Here, between the Rhine and the Danube, Vespasian acquired peaceful possession of territory, which from the payment of tithes as rental by colonists who settled there was called the *Agri Decumates*. The *Germania* of Tacitus contains comparatively little geography, but shows considerable knowledge of the peoples. There is a good account [3] of the Rhine and the Danube, but no mention

[1] *Agric.*, 11.   [2] *Ibid.*, 24.   [3] *Germ.*, 1.

of the Vistula. This work, however, contains the earliest reference to the Angli [1] and the Fenni [2] (the Finns) and describes the "states of the Suiones" (Sweden) as lying in the ocean.[3] The Romans were beginning to know something about the coast of the Baltic Sea. In this connection it may be noted that Pliny [4] tells a story of a Roman knight who in the reign of Nero was sent out to find amber and traveled as far as the shore of the northern ocean, 600 miles from Carnuntum in Pannonia. He brought back a great quantity of amber, but, so far as Pliny tells us, no information about the country. The amber trade was probably following the course that it had always followed, along the valley of the Vistula.

Besides Britain the only important addition to the Roman domain during this period was the province of Dacia, north of the Danube, which was organized by the emperor Trajan. The province was abandoned by Aurelian in 274.

In the east the Euphrates was not crossed by a Roman army between the reign of Augustus and that of Trajan. In 114 Trajan organized Armenia and northern Mesopotamia as Roman provinces and, two years later, formed the province of Assyria beyond the Tigris. This newly acquired territory was all abandoned by Hadrian. During this period India was constantly becoming better known through traders, and a voyage undertaken probably in the first half of the first century made communication permanently easier. A Greek named Hippalus first

[1] *Germ.*, 40.   [2] *Ibid.*, 46.   [3] *Ibid.*, 44.   [4] *N. H.*, xxxvii, 11 (45).

had the courage to sail straight from the promontory of Syagros (Cape Fartak in southern Arabia) to the west coast of India.[1] He could thus take advantage of the monsoon, and this became the regular practice.

Ancient Chinese chronicles record the arrival of envoys from the Roman emperor Antun (Marcus Aurelius) in 166, an interesting but not very satisfying side-light upon Roman relations with the Far East.[2]

In Nero's reign two centurions were sent up the Nile to find its source, — one of the few instances in antiquity of an expedition for the sole purpose of exploration. Pliny [3] and Seneca [4] give some account of the expedition, and Seneca says that he got his information from two members of the party. He speaks of marshes above the junction of the White Nile and the Blue Nile in nine degrees north latitude, a region that was first visited again in 1839–1840. About the same time, in western Africa, Suetonius Paulinus, who was then governor of Mauretania, marched into the interior — the first to carry Roman arms across Mount Atlas — and brought back a great deal of information about the country and its people.[5]

After the reign of Trajan the emperors added nothing either to the imperial domain or to geographical knowledge.

[1] Pliny, N. H., vi, 26 (100–101); Periplus Mare Eryth., 57.
[2] Yule, Cathay and the Way Thither, I, 62.
[3] N. H., vi, 35 (184–186).   [4] Quaest. Nat., vi, 8.
[5] Pliny, N. H., v, 1 (14–15).

XVIII. *Pliny*

GAIUS PLINIUS SECUNDUS, commonly known as the
older Pliny, was born at Comum in northern Italy
in A.D. 23. In spite of constant occupation in military
service or as provincial governor, he found time to
read extensively and to gather an astonishing amount
of information on various subjects, including geography. His only surviving work, the *Natural History*, is in thirty-seven books, and, though lacking
in critical judgment, is a mine of information on
many subjects. This was published in 77. Pliny
died at Stabiae during the eruption of Vesuvius in
79, at which time he was commander of the fleet at
Misenum.

The geographical part of his work is contained in
books iii, iv, v, and vi. In describing the earth he
begins at the Pillars of Hercules and follows the
northern coast of the Mediterranean to the river
Tanais, digressing at convenient points to describe
the islands of the western Mediterranean, the countries of central Europe, and the Greek islands. After
speaking of the Scythians and the Hyperboreans, he
crosses the Rhipaean Mountains to the northern
ocean and returns by the northern and western coasts
of Europe to Gades, giving a little information about
Britain and Ireland, and more about the western
coasts of Gaul and Spain.

Pliny's knowledge of the countries of central
Europe is better than that of earlier writers. He
knows the tributaries of the Danube and rejects the

notion that there is a branch flowing into the Adriatic.[1] In his account of the northern ocean he mentions [2] the *Codanus Sinus* (the Baltic Sea) and several large islands there, — Baltia, Raunonia, where amber was cast up by the sea in the spring, and Scandinavia (the Codannovia of Mela), which was said by its inhabitants to form a second world. He knows also the Cimbric Chersonesus.[3] In connection with Britain, which, he says, was formerly called Albion, he mentions [4] the Orcades, the Acmodae (the Shetland Islands), and the Haebudes (the Hebrides). He speaks of an island Monapia, probably the Isle of Man.[5] In view of the popular conception of the location of the Cassiterides, which Pliny, like others, connects with Spain,[6] it is interesting to note that he refers [7] to a statement of Timaeus, who lived three centuries earlier, regarding a tin island called Mictis, which has been identified by some with Saint Michaels Mount near the southwestern corner of Britain, by others with Cornwall; some have thought that Mictis is an error for Vectis, the Isle of Wight.

In his treatment of Gaul the description of the peninsula of Brittany is surprisingly accurate.[8] The account of Spain, however, is somewhat unsatisfactory, though Pliny had been governor there. He even confuses the promontory near Lisbon, which was called by Mela the *Promunturium Magnum*, with the Celtic Promontory at the northwest corner, thus

[1] iii, 22 (127).   [2] iv, 27 (94–96); xxxvii, 11 (35).
[3] iv, 27 (96).   [4] *Ibid.*, 30 (102–103).   [5] *Ibid.*, 30 (103).
[6] *Ibid.*, 36 (119).   [7] *Ibid.*, 30 (104).   [8] *Ibid.*, 32 (107).

88   DISCOVERY OF THE ANCIENT WORLD

making all the western coast of Spain north of the
Tagus face toward the north.[1]

Having finished his description of Europe, he starts
again at the Pillars of Hercules and follows the northern coast of Africa, digressing when he reaches Egypt
to tell what he knows of the interior. He is perhaps
the first to mention the river Niger,[2] though there is
a question whether the river which he calls Nigris is
the one now known as the Niger. There is no indication that he had seen Hanno's narrative of his voyage
along the western coast. He describes Egypt and the
Nile in great detail and refers to the exploration of
Ethiopia and the upper Nile by the officers sent by
Nero.[3] He had no conception of the great southern
extension of the continent, but thought that the
southern coast began at a point near the entrance to
the Red Sea. In fact he states definitely that it is
generally agreed that the southern ocean is 625 miles
south of Meroe.[4]

From the mouth of the Nile the account follows the
Mediterranean coast to the Gulf of Issus, with a di-
gression on the interior of Asia as far as the Euphrates, of which there is an excellent detailed description. There follows a description of Asia Minor
and the neighboring islands, the course continuing
along the Euxine to Lake Maeotis. Proceeding now
toward the east, the author discusses the Caspian Sea
and the surrounding regions and continues through
the land of the Scythians to the eastern ocean. Quot-

[1] iv, 35 (113).
[2] v, 8 (44).
[3] vi, 35 (184–186).
[4] Ibid., 35 (196).

ing from Varro, he gives the course of the overland
trade-route from India to the Euxine, — through
Bactria, down the river Icarus (not elsewhere mentioned) to the Oxus, and down the Oxus to the Caspian; thence up the river Cyrus, overland to the
Phasis, and down that river to the Euxine.[1] He mentions several rivers in the country of the Seres, whom,
like Mela, he locates on the eastern ocean between
Tabis and India.[2] The island called Chryse in Mela's
geography becomes a promontory in Pliny's work.[3]
The eastern coast of India, according to Pliny, is a
straight line from Mount Emodus, a part of the
Taurus ranges, to the point where the coast turns to
the west.[4] He describes the Ganges [5] and the Indus [6]
in detail and mentions several places in India not
found in earlier writers. He gives the various routes
to India and describes the whole trip from Alexandria
to Muziris on the western coast of India, by way of
Coptos and Berenice.[7]

In the reign of Claudius a man sailing around
Arabia was driven by the wind all the way to Taprobane (Ceylon). After he had remained there for some
months, the king sent him back to Rome and sent
four envoys with him. From these men Pliny got
much new information about the island, though he
still clings to the old idea regarding its size and its
distance from the mainland. He says that it is 1,000
miles long and four days' sail from India; in fact, the
dimensions are about 240 by 138 miles, and it is

[1] vi, 19 (52).   [2] Ibid., 20 (54).   [3] Ibid., 20 (55).
[4] Ibid., 21 (56).   [5] Ibid., 22 (65–69).
[6] Ibid., 23 (72).   [7] Ibid., 26 (96–106).

about 69 miles from the mainland. He makes the interesting statement that the inhabitants trade with the Seres, the earliest indication that we have of the existence of trade along the coast of the eastern ocean.[1]

From the mouth of the Indus Pliny's account follows the coast to the west, including a description of Parthia, Mesopotamia, the river Tigris, Arabia, and, finally, the region between the Red Sea and the Nile, with a full treatment of Ethiopia. His geography ends with a discussion of comparative distances and the division of the earth's surface by means of parallels.

XIX. *The Periplus of the Erythraean Sea*

IN A manuscript in Heidelberg there is a peculiar and, from a geographical point of view, most important work entitled *A Periplus of the Erythraean Sea*.[2] The unknown author was a Greek from Alexandria. The work was probably written in the latter part of the first century. It is a guide-book, a manual for navigators, describing the coasts of the Red Sea, the eastern coast of Africa to a point below the equator, the coast of Arabia, and the western coast of India, with some interesting references to the more remote parts of India and even China. It contains also much information about harbors and exports and imports.

The first part of the work describes the route south from Myoshormos along the western coast of the Red Sea, with information about the ports of Berenice,

---

[1] vi, 24 (84–91).   [2] Mueller, *Geog. Graec. Min.*, vol. i.

Ptolemais (the station for the elephant-hunters of the Ptolemies), and Adulis, the chief place of export for Ethiopia. The route is then continued outside the Strait of Bab-el-Mandeb to Avelites, Malao, Mundus, Mosyllum, the Elephant Promontory, and the Aromata Promontory (Cape Guardafui), the easternmost point of the African continent.

The author of the *Periplus* is the first who shows any knowledge of the great southern extension of Africa, though undoubtedly there had been trade for a long time up and down the eastern coast. The places that are mentioned south of the Aromata Promontory can be identified with reasonable certainty. Opone is the first, about ninety miles to the south, and beyond, according to the author, the voyage continues for six days, at first due south and then southwest along a coast that is marked by cliffs. Then there are six days along a sandy shore. From this point it is a journey of seven days along Azania to the Pyralaan Islands. From here the course continues for two days to Manuthias, an island thirty miles from the mainland (probably Pemba or Zanzibar), and two days farther to Rhapta, an important trading-place. Beyond this nothing is known.

We have here, therefore, a description of the eastern coast of Africa to a point about six degrees south of the equator, some 1,500 miles south of Cape Guardafui. Ptolemy's knowledge extended only a little farther.

The writer now starts again [1] at Leuce Come on the

[1] *Periplus*, 19.

Red Sea and follows the eastern coast toward the south. Sailors avoided this side, he says, because the coast was rocky and the natives were barbarous. The chief trading-post was Muza, just inside the Strait of Bab-el-Mandeb. From here, a journey of twelve days inland, was Saphar, the capital of the Homeritae and the Sabaei. In the narrowest part of the strait was Ocelis and, farther on, outside the strait, was Adana (Aden). Beyond was a barren sandy coast as far as Cane. The capital of this region was Sabatha in the interior. Beyond Cane was a gulf, with the promontory Syagros (Fartak) at its eastern extremity. The author is at fault here; the gulf is east of Syagros, not west. It was at this place that vessels going to India struck out into the open sea.

The account from this point to the mouth of the Indus is less detailed. The author mentions the important town of Moscha, just west of Syagros, and the island of Sarapis, gives a clear description of the entrance to the Persian Gulf, and speaks of towns at its head. He then continues his voyage along the coast of Carmania and Gedrosia to the seven mouths of the Indus. He mentions a town here, Barbarice, and beyond, a deep bay called Eirinon. Still farther on is another bay and the important city of Barygaza, from which are exported goods from the interior of India and silk from China.

From Barygaza the journey continues [1] to the south along the western coast of India to Muziris and Nelcynda, the precise location of which places it is

_____
[1] *Periplus*, 50.

impossible to determine. The author says that ships made the voyage from Ocelis in Arabia to Muziris, somewhat more than 2,000 miles, in forty days. Nelcynda was one of the chief trading places on this coast, and it is interesting to note that some of the things which were exported had been brought from Chryse. The writer gives incidentally some information about the interior of India. He speaks of deserts and high mountains, of nations extending as far as the Ganges, and of several cities of doubtful location.

The description of the coast from Nelcynda to the mouth of the Ganges is apparently based upon hearsay rather than upon the author's own observation. He mentions the promontory Comari (Cape Comorin), but, instead of turning to the east at that point, erroneously continues south to Colchi. Here, he says, there is a gulf with a headland on the farther side, which is regarded by the author as the end of the western coast, but is in fact on the eastern coast. Modern geographers have identified this headland with Cape Calimere. The people of this region are said to have carried on trade with Chryse and with places at the mouth of the Ganges.

The author of the *Periplus* thought that Ceylon was all south of India and that it extended far to the west.[1] He calls the island Palaesimundus, which was the name of its chief city. From the promontory opposite Ceylon which the author regarded as the southern point of India, the course continues up the eastern coast to the mouth of the Ganges, but the

[1] *Periplus*, 61,

description is meagre. Chryse is located opposite the mouth of the Ganges and is said to be the most remote of all lands in the east. It is usually identified with the Malay Peninsula.

One of the most interesting things in the *Periplus* is a reference to the city of Thina in the interior, in the country of the Thinae.[1] The name is probably the same as that of the Sinae of Ptolemy, who says that they lived south of the Seres. These are the earliest allusions to China. There is no reference to communication by sea with this country, but, according to the *Periplus*, silk was exported from there either through Bactria or down the Ganges. There is an allusion also to a neighboring people called the Sessatae, who are not mentioned elsewhere. Beyond them the country is said to be inaccessible on account of the severe cold.

XX. *Marinus of Tyre*

THOUGH the work of Marinus has not been preserved, it is important in the history of ancient geography, because it was one of the chief authorities for Ptolemy. Ptolemy himself frankly acknowledges [2] his indebtedness and constantly refers to his predecessor. In fact, without these references we should know nothing about Marinus. He lived probably in the first half of the second century and was primarily a mathematical geographer, the successor of Eratosthenes and Hipparchus. Our interest in him lies

---

[1] *Periplus*, 64–65.   [2] i, 6.

mainly in the fact that his work, as quoted by Ptolemy, shows a surprising advance in the geographical knowledge of Asia and Africa.

Hipparchus had undertaken to make a map of the world on a scientific basis, determining latitude and longitude by astronomical observations. Marinus was the first to undertake again the same task, but the information at his disposal was little better than that of his predecessor and his results were often quite inaccurate. In fact he often had to resort to the old-fashioned method of computing distances by the number of days' journeys, and, if the result was obviously impossible, he would arbitrarily alter the figure.

At the northern limit of the known world Marinus placed Thule in 63 degrees north latitude, identifying it with the Shetland Islands, which are actually in 60 degrees north latitude.[1] This had come to be the common idea regarding Thule. Though he was mistaken concerning both their latitude and longitude, he placed the Fortunate Islands correctly further west than the Sacred Promontory in Spain, which had hitherto been considered the most western point in the inhabited world, and from them he reckoned his longitude.[2] In general, his map was distorted in many ways; both the length and breadth of the known world were enormously exaggerated.

Marinus was the first to recognize the great extension of Asia toward the east. He gave an itinerary of a Macedonian silk-merchant from the Euphrates to Sera, the capital of the Seres, estimating the distances

[1] Ptol., i, 7, 1.   [2] Ibid., 12, 11.

in parasangs.[1] The route passed through Bactria and then toward the northeast to the western slope of the mountains called Emodae; then through a mountainous country to a deep, ascending valley, at the top of which was a place named Stone Tower, from which the mountains extended to the east until they joined the chain of Imaus. Beyond the Stone Tower no details were given, but it was said to be a journey of seven months (about 4,200 miles) from there to Sera. The course probably followed the upper valley of the river Oxus, and the lack of details for the latter part of the route was due to the fact that the silk was taken from the Seres at their western frontier.

The statements of Marinus regarding southeastern Asia indicate an enormous advance in the geographical knowledge of that part of the world. He was, however, absolutely incorrect in his conception of India, giving it a long southern coast line with only a slight extension toward the south. The *Periplus of the Erythraean Sea* had shown an approximately accurate knowledge of the great peninsula, and it is difficult to understand why Marinus departed from this correct conception. The cities of India that he mentioned, Curula and Palura, though they cannot be identified, were undoubtedly on the eastern coast.[2] He was the first to record the existence of the Gulf of the Ganges, the width of which he estimated at about 1,500 miles.[3] He was the first also to give definite information regarding lands east of India. On the eastern side of the Gulf of the Ganges he mentioned

[1] Ptol., i, 11, 4 ff.   [2] *Ibid.*, 13, 4 ff.   [3] *Ibid.*, 13, 7.

the city of Sada and, 400 miles southeast of this, Tamala.[1] Beyond this, 185 miles in the same direction, he placed the Golden Chersonesus (the Malay Peninsula), the Chryse of earlier geographers.[2] From this point he quoted a man named Alexander to the effect that it was a journey of twenty days along a coast facing south to the city of Zabae, and then, for a vessel sailing east, a voyage of "some days" to Cattigara, which he located about 5,800 miles east of the southern point of India.[3] This city, evidently an important one, was placed by Ptolemy at the southeastern limit of the world.

It is obvious that, though they knew of the existence of lands beyond the Malay Peninsula, neither Marinus nor Ptolemy knew anything of their geography. By his exaggeration of the length of Asia from west to east Marinus made the inhabited world extend two-thirds of the way around the globe, which, following Posidonius, he conceived as having a circumference of only about 20,750 miles. So far as the evidence goes, he did not assume the existence of an eastern ocean.

During the reign of Augustus the Romans had reached the country of the Garamantes in northern Africa south of the Lesser Syrtis, had established friendly relations with the rulers of the country, and were permitted to use the oasis as a basis for further exploration. Later expeditions of the first century were recorded by Marinus. He said that Septimius Flaccus, governor of Africa, after a march of three

[1] Ptol., i, 13, 8.   [2] Ibid., 13, 9.   [3] Ibid., 14, 1 ff.

months to the south, reached the land of the Ethiopians. Later, Julius Maternus, setting out from
Garama, the principal town of the Garamantes, journeyed for four months to the south and arrived in a
country of the Ethiopians called Agisymba, a name
used by Ptolemy in a general sense of central Africa
south of the desert.[1] On the basis of days' journeys
Marinus calculated that the expedition reached a
point about 2,840 miles south of the equator, but,
realizing that this was impossible, he arbitrarily reduced his estimate by more than one-half.[2] In the
same absurd fashion he reckoned the latitude of his
southern limit on the eastern coast, the promontory
of Prasum, and came to the conclusion that Maternus
reached a point in the same latitude as Prasum.[3] The
expedition probably got as far as the region between
the Niger and Lake Tchad, in about fourteen degrees
north latitude.

XXI. *Ptolemy*

CLAUDIUS PTOLEMAEUS lived at Alexandria in the
second century after Christ. Beyond this, nothing is
known about his life. He was primarily an astronomer and most of his extant writings are on the subjects of astronomy or astrology. His geographical
work, in eight books, is an attempt to carry out the
dictum of Hipparchus, that a reliable map could be
constructed only by observations of latitude and
longitude, and the larger part of it consists of mere

---

[1] Ptol., i, 8, 5; iv, 9, 5.   [2] *Ibid.*, 8, 3; 14, 6.   [3] *Ibid.*, 8, 2; 9, 3–4.

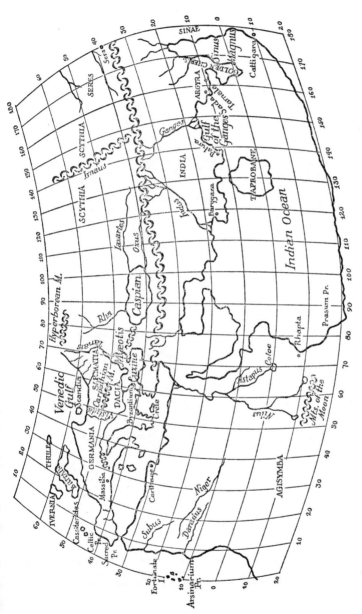

THE WORLD ACCORDING TO PTOLEMY

lists of places with their supposed latitude and longitude. Included in the work is a general map of the world and there are twenty-six others showing details. On his general map Ptolemy sought to reproduce on a flat surface the contour of the globe by representing the parallels and meridians as curved lines; on the smaller maps they appear as straight lines. In two manuscripts the maps are said to be the work of Agathodaemon of Alexandria, but there is no evidence as to his identity or date. He may have been employed by Ptolemy to make the maps or he may have been a later copyist. Whoever made them, the maps in the manuscripts may be regarded as representing Ptolemy's geographical conceptions.

Though the author gives the impression that his statements are based upon astronomical observations, he had in fact precise information about very few places and had to depend largely upon itineraries, days' journeys, and so forth. Centuries before, Pytheas had determined the latitude of Massilia; besides this, only Alexandria, Rhodes, Rome, and the Strait of Gibraltar could be placed with approximate accuracy. For determining longitude there was no practical method. Thus, Ptolemy's latitude is often incorrect and his longitude is even more at fault. He exaggerates the width of the inhabited world from north to south, but his error in the length from east to west is far greater, with the result that the interval between western Europe and eastern Asia is much less than it should be. Since Ptolemy was the chief geographical authority of the fifteenth century, it was this mistaken conception on his part which encouraged Columbus to sail from Spain in the hope of reaching the Asiatic coast.

The distortion of Ptolemy's map is due partly to the fact that, like Marinus of Tyre, he abandoned the estimate of Eratosthenes regarding the circumference of the globe and adopted that of Posidonius, which is less than the actual circumference by nearly 5,000 miles. Thus, his parallels and meridians were too close together and a given distance would cover too many degrees on his map. Moreover, again following Marinus, he selected as a starting-point for his system of longitude the meridian passing through the outermost of the Fortunate Islands, and he was mistaken by about seven degrees in his idea of the distance of those islands from the mainland.

Though his knowledge of the inhabited world is more extensive than that of any earlier geographer, with the possible exception of Marinus, his information about details is in many respects less accurate. On the western coast of Spain he puts the Sacred Promontory incorrectly farther west than the Celtic Promontory (Cape Finisterre) and does not mention the very prominent headland called the Rock of Lisbon, which is farther west than either of the other projections.[1] The Cassiterides he places off the coast of Spain near Finisterre, where there are no islands.[2] On the Gallic coast he makes the peninsula of Brittany too small and does not mention the peninsula in

[1] ii, 5, 2; 7, 2.   [2] Ibid., 6, 76.

Normandy. Lutetia (Paris) he places opposite the mouth of the Loire.[1]

He is incorrect regarding the latitude and longitude of Britain and is quite mistaken as to its shape. He is, to be sure, better informed about the southern part of the island than the northern part. Strangely enough, beyond the Tyne and the Solway he makes it extend east and west, putting the northern end of Scotland farther south than the promontory Novantum (Galloway in southwestern Scotland). That is, the whole of Scotland is made to run east and west instead of north and south.[2] Though he puts Ireland, which he calls Ivernia, too far north, his knowledge of it is much more detailed than that of any earlier writer.[3] He gives a *periplus* of the island, mentioning seven towns in the interior and two on the coast, including Eblana (Dublin). Several of the rivers in Ireland that he names can be identified.

During the past century the Romans had apparently added little to their knowledge of Germany. Ptolemy mentions [4] for the first time the Saxones and gives approximately the correct dimensions for the Cimbric Chersonesus.[5] If we admit a slight emendation of the text,[6] he locates the Suiones on the coast of Germany; Scandinavia appears as Scandia, an island of moderate size.[7] The Vistula is the eastern boundary of Germany and beyond is Sarmatia.[8] Ptolemy's statement regarding the coast that extends toward the east from the mouth of the Vistula indi-

---

[1] ii, 7, 1; 8, 13.   [2] *Ibid.*, 3, 1.   [3] *Ibid.*, 2.
[4] *Ibid.*, 11, 11.   [5] *Ibid.*, 11, 2.   [6] *Ibid.*, 11, 16.
[7] *Ibid.*, 11, 34–35.   [8] viii, 10, 2.

cates some knowledge of the east coast of the Baltic
Sea, though of course, since he had no information
about Scandinavia, he did not realize that it was an
enclosed sea. He conceives the coast as extending
east and then northeast and says that the bay thus
formed is called the Venedic Gulf, named from the
Venedi, a Sarmatian tribe.[1] Roman conquests and
the recent occupation of the country north and south
of the Danube had increased the geographical knowledge of this region. Ptolemy knows the Carpathian
Mountains [2] between Dacia and Sarmatia and mentions four rivers flowing into the northern ocean,
none of which can be identified.[3]

He puts the Euxine too far north and is incorrect
about the rivers flowing into it.[4] As so many other
geographers had done, he exaggerates enormously
the size of the Maeotis, putting its northern limit
almost as far north as the southern coast of the Baltic
Sea,[5] thus making the Maeotis serve as a large part
of the boundary between European and Asiatic Sarmatia, and throwing the river Tanais into the far
north. Between the Maeotis and the Baltic he puts
the Rhipaean Mountains, and the Hyperborean
Mountains he places still further north at the limit
of the known world.[6] Here he puts the source of the
river Rha (the Volga), which he regards as the eastern
boundary of the Asiatic Sarmatians and of which he
gives the first definite information.[7] In his conception of the Caspian Sea he returns to the opinion of

[1] iii, 5, 1.   [2] *Ibid.*, 5, 6; 8, 1.   [3] *Ibid.*, 5, 2.
[4] *Ibid.*, 5, 7.   [5] *Ibid.*, 6, 4.
[6] *Ibid.*, 5, 15, 22; v, 9, 13.   [7] v, 9, 12–13.

Herodotus, that it is an inland sea, not connected with the northern ocean. But he underestimates its size and believes that its greater length is east and west.[1]

There are many errors, even in the position of the Mediterranean countries, due to mistakes in latitude and longitude. The Mediterranean Sea is too long [2] and especially in the western part is too wide. There is no knowledge of the projection of Africa to the north, extending from Carthage to the Strait of Gibraltar. Sardinia and Carthage are nearly three degrees too far south,[3] and Byzantium is in the same latitude as Massilia.[4] Italy extends too far to the east and is then carried to the south. In Greece Taenarum is too far south, with the result that Crete appears between the Peloponnesus and southwestern Asia Minor.[5]

In Asia the Taurus ranges are regarded as the backbone of the whole continent. Another chain of mountains, extending north and south and separating eastern and western Scythia, is called Imaus, formerly the name of a part of the Taurus ranges.[6] Of the region east of the Volga and north of the Iaxartes Ptolemy has no knowledge, though he gives the names of tribes, some real and some mythical. He appears to consider Scythia as unlimited on the north and east. He mentions fifteen towns of the Seres, including the capital, Sera, the distance of which from the Stone Tower, as given by Marinus, he arbitrarily reduces

[1] vii, 5, 4.   [2] i, 12, 11–12.   [3] iii, 3; iv, 3, 7.
[4] ii, 10, 8; iii, 11, 5.   [5] i, 12, 11.   [6] vi, 13, 1; 14, 1.

by one-half. He gives the names also of mountains
and rivers in the country of the Seres, but he seems
not to have realized that the rivers must flow into the
eastern ocean.[1] South of the Seres he speaks of the
Sinae and the Golden Chersonesus.[2] The country
of the Sinae, who were undoubtedly the Chinese,
would correspond with what is now southern China.

Ptolemy follows Marinus in his incorrect conception of India, extending it only four degrees to the
south of Barygaza and giving it a long southern
coast line.[3] For the Gulf of the Ganges he claims to
have older and better authorities than Marinus.[4] He
mentions Palura at the southwestern corner of the
gulf, the point where the voyage to the Golden
Chersonesus began.[5] On the east side of the gulf, in a
region which he calls the Land of Silver, are the cities
Sada and Tamala.[6] East of the Golden Chersonesus
he mentions a great gulf (the Gulf of Siam), and, beyond this, are the Sinae and their important trading-
post, Cattigara, at the southeastern corner of Asia.[7]
Ptolemy seems to assume that the land of the Sinae
extends without limit toward the east and that this
coast on which he locates Cattigara faces west and
extends toward the south. In other words, he under-
stands that the coast beyond the Gulf of Siam extends
to the south rather than to the north. In fact he believed that this coast was prolonged to the south and
then to the west until it joined the eastern coast of
Africa near the promontory of Prasum. The Indian

[1] i, 11, 4–5; 12, 1–3; vi, 13, 2; vi, 16.   [2] vii, 2; 4.
[3] vii, 1, 9–11.   [4] i, 17, 5.
[5] *Ibid.*, 13, 7; vii, 1, 15.   [6] vii, 2, 3, 17.   [7] *Ibid.*, 2, 7; 3, 3.

Ocean thus became, according to Ptolemy, an inland sea.[1]

Like earlier geographers he exaggerates the size of Ceylon, making it about fourteen times as large as it actually is. This is surprising, since he gives a *periplus* of the island, mentioning tribes, towns, and so forth.[2]

On the east coast of Africa Ptolemy places the town of Rhapta, which had been mentioned in the *Periplus of the Erythraean Sea*, in seven degrees south latitude, and, beyond this, following Marinus, he speaks of a great bay extending to a promontory called Prasum in fifteen and a half degrees south latitude.[3] In his detailed description of the Nile he states that it is formed by two rivers flowing from two lakes a little south of the equator.[4] These are the Victoria and the Albert Nyanza. Knowledge of these lakes, which were rediscovered in the nineteenth century, had been brought by traders to the eastern coast. Ptolemy speaks also of Lake Coloe, called by Strabo [5] Lake Psebo, the source of the river Astapus [6] (the Blue Nile). This is Lake Tzana in Abyssinia. South of the lakes which are the sources of the Nile he places the Mountains of the Moon.[7] He mentions rivers in central Africa, one of which may be the Niger, though the identification is very doubtful.[8] For the western coast of northern Africa his latitude and longitude are quite incorrect and the results are confusing. He thinks that the coast extends south instead of south-

[1] vii, 3, 6.
[2] *Ibid.*, 4.
[3] iv, 7, 12; 8, 1.
[4] *Ibid.*, 7, 23–24.
[5] xvii, 1, 3.
[6] Ptol., iv, 8, 24.
[7] *Ibid.*, 8, 3.
[8] *Ibid.*, 6, 14.

west. He mentions a mountain at the end of the main chain of Atlas, a river called Subus, and another called Daradus, which he places in fifteen degrees north latitude.[1] This river would naturally be identified with the Draa or Drah, the mouth of which is in twenty-eight degrees north latitude. Farther south is the promontory of Arsinarium and opposite this, much too far south, he places the Fortunate Islands.[2]

XXII. *Conclusion*

WITH Ptolemy the story of the discovery of the ancient world comes to an end. We have traced the gradual extension of geographical knowledge until in the second century it embraced those parts of Europe, Asia, and Africa which are described with more or less accuracy by Ptolemy. In antiquity these limits were not extended. So far as we know, there were no more voyages or expeditions for the purpose of exploration, there were no military campaigns which penetrated regions that were still unknown, and, though traders in remote parts of the world may have become familiar with parts still more remote, there is no record of their increased knowledge.

Books in Greek or Latin on the subject of geography written after the middle of the second century contain little or no new information. There is still in existence a Greek poem of about 1,200 verses, with the title *A Description (Periegesis) of the Inhabited World*.[6] The author, whose date is quite doubtful,

---

[1] iv, 1, 4; 6, 6; 6, 8.   [2] *Ibid.*, 6, 6; 6, 34.
[3] Mueller, *Geog. Graec. Min.*, vol. II.

was Dionysius Periegetes, the surname coming from the title of his work. Though the poem has little geographical value, it appears to have been very popular in the later empire. There were paraphrases of it in Greek prose and two poetical translations in Latin, one by Avienus, written in the fourth century, and one by Priscian, of the sixth century; also a full commentary by Eustathius, written in the twelfth century. In the latter part of the third century Solinus wrote his *Memorabilia*, better known by the title of a later edition, *Polyhistor*. This contains much geographical material of little value, drawn chiefly from Pliny. It was widely read, however, and by later writers was used instead of Pliny. In the fourth century Ammianus Marcellinus wrote his history of the Roman emperors in thirty-one books. Of these the last eighteen survive and, as the author appreciated the connection between geography and history, they contain much geographical material, especially with reference to the manners and customs of remote peoples, — the Huns (first mentioned by Dionysius Periegetes), the Saracens, and so forth. Besides his translation of the poem of Dionysius, we have a long fragment of another work by Avienus,[1] in which he describes the coast outside the Pillars of Hercules and the Mediterranean coast from Gades to Massilia, and mentions the voyage of the Carthaginian, Himilco, who, according to Pliny,[2] explored the western coast of Europe while Hanno was sailing along the western coast of Africa.

[1] Mueller, *op. cit.*, vol. ii.   [2] *N. H.*, ii, 67.

The Itineraries which are still in existence date from the fourth century. The publication of these began in the reign of Augustus and was continued by the later emperors. They were official lists of stopping-places on the roads of the empire, with a statement of distances. We have two *Itineraria Antonini*, compiled in their original form under Caracalla and revised in the reign of Diocletian. One of these contains Europe, Asia, and Africa; the other gives sea-routes. We have also the so-called *Jerusalem Itinerary*, an account of a pilgrimage from Burdigala (Bordeaux) to Jerusalem by way of Milan, Aquileia, and Constantinople, with the return by way of Brundisium, Rome, and Milan. There is, finally, the *Itinerarium Alexandri*, an account of the expedition of Alexander the Great, dedicated to the emperor Constantius II on the occasion of his expedition against the Persians.

In the fifth century a Gaul named Rutilius visited Rome and described his return voyage in two books of elegiac verse, of which we have the first and a part of the second. There are some details not found in the geographers and he is the only Latin writer who describes Ilva and other islands off the western coast of Italy.

With the exception of Ptolemy's maps, the only map of the imperial period which is still in existence is the so-called *Tabula Peutingeriana*, a copy of a map made in the third or fourth century. This copy was made in the thirteenth century and gets its name from the fact that Konrad Peutinger of Augsburg secured it in 1508 from its discoverer, Konrad Celtes. It is now in Vienna. The natural geographical features and provincial boundaries of the original map were probably based upon Agrippa's map in the *Porticus Vipsania*, the network of roads being an addition. The existing copy was painted in colors on twelve sheets of parchment pasted together in a strip about twenty-three feet long and a little more than a foot wide. The sheet at the left, containing Spain and most of Britain, has disappeared. It is obvious from the dimensions that this is not a map of the world in the usual sense; it does, however, pretend to represent the world as it was known to the Romans, but with all distances from north to south greatly reduced and those from east to west exaggerated. The result is, of course, absurd distortion. The peculiar form of the map, however, is not due to ignorance. It is really only a road-map and would serve that purpose fairly well, since the relative positions of towns and the distances between them are given with some accuracy.

Ptolemy, the last of the geographical scholars of antiquity, was the one most highly regarded in the Middle Ages and at the time of the revival of learning, partly because he represented the world approximately as it was known for many centuries, partly because his work was provided with maps, and partly on account of its scientific form, unreliable as that was. The Arabians were great travelers and in their writings often referred to Ptolemy and even wrote books based upon his. But his geographical work became well known in western Europe only when it was translated into Latin in 1409. As the new intellectual era progressed and as a vigorous interest in maritime discovery developed, Ptolemy was considered the great authority on geography. A Latin translation was printed without maps in 1475 and an edition with maps appeared three years later. Many editions were printed in the sixteenth century and, as knowledge of the world increased, the maps were gradually extended and corrected. It was only when the development of science and the discovery of new lands had made his calculations and maps obsolete that the last of the ancient geographers ceased to be an authority.

BIBLIOGRAPHY

BIBLIOGRAPHY

The following is a list of some of the more recent books which would be useful to a student of ancient geography. It is by no means exhaustive. With a few exceptions, articles in periodicals, many of them of much value, have not been included.

I

Modern Works of a more or less comprehensive nature, listed in the Order of Publication

NIEBUHR, B. G. Lectures on Ancient Ethnography and Geography; translated from the German. 2 vols. Boston, 1854.

SMITH, W. Dictionary of Greek and Roman Geography. 2 vols. Boston, 1854–57.

VIVIEN DE SAINT-MARTIN, L. Histoire de la Géographie et des Découvertes Géographiques. Paris, 1873–74.

FORBIGER, A. Handbuch der Alten Geographie. 3 vols. Hamburg, 1877.

KIEPERT, H. Lehrbuch der Alten Geographie. Berlin, 1878.

BUNBURY, E. H. A History of Ancient Geography. 2 vols. London, 1883.

NORDENSKIÖLD, A. E. Facsimile-Atlas to the Early History of Cartography; translated from the Swedish. Stockholm, 1889.

TOZER, H. F. History of Ancient Geography. Cambridge, England, 1897.

MILLER, K. Die Ältesten Weltkarten, vol. VI. Stuttgart, 1898.

MÜLLER, C. Studien zur Geschichte der Erdkunde im Altertum. Breslau, 1902.

BERGER, E. H. Geschichte der Wissenschaftlichen Erdkunde der Griechen. Leipzig, 1903.

KELTIE, J. S., and HOWARTH, O. J. R. History of Geography. London, 1913.

KENDE, O. Handbuch der Geographischen Wissenschaft. Berlin, 1914.

BESNIER, M. Lexique de Géographie Ancienne. Paris, 1914.

ALMAGIA, R. La Geographia nell' Età Classica. Novara, 1915.

Cambridge Ancient History; edited by J. S. Bury and others. Cambridge, England, 1923–30.

DAUNT, H. D. The Centre of Ancient Civilization; Discoveries in Ancient Geography and Mythologies. London, 1926.

CARY, M., and WARMINGTON, E. H. The Ancient Explorers. London, 1929.

BAKER, J. N. L. A History of Geographical Discovery and Exploration. London, 1931.

SEMPLE, ELLEN C. The Geography of the Mediterranean Region. New York, 1931.

II

The Ancient Geographers, Other Works in Greek or Latin containing Geographical Material, and Modern Interpretations or Discussions of these; listed in the Chronological Order of the Classical Authors

MURRAY, A. T. The Iliad and the Odyssey of Homer, with an English translation. Loeb Classical Library. London, 1919–25.

LANG, G. Untersuchungen zur Geographie der Odyssee. Karlsruhe, 1905.

LANG, A. The World of Homer. London, 1910.

ALLEN, T. W. The Homeric Catalogue of Ships. Oxford, 1921.

DÖRPFELD, W. and RÜTER, H. Homers Odyssee, die Wiederherstellung des Ursprünglichen Epos von der Heimkehr des Odysseus. Munich, 1925.

BÉRARD, V. Les Phéniciens et l'Odyssée. 2 vols. Paris, 1927.

EVELYN-WHITE, H. G. Hesiod, The Homeric Hymns, and Homerica; with an English translation. Loeb Classical Library. London, 1914.

GISINGER, F. Zur Geographie bei Hesiod. Rheinisches Museum, 1929.

TOURNIER, E. De Aristea Proconnesio et Arimaspeo Poemate. Paris, 1863.

TROPEA, G. Ecateo ed i Fragmenti della Periegesis. Messina, 1896–97.

JACOBY, F. Fragmente der Griechischen Historiker, vol. I. Berlin, 1923. (For the Fragments of Hecataeus.)

FISCHER, C. T. De Hannonis Periplo. Leipzig, 1893.

SCHOFF, W. H. The Periplus of Hanno; with translation and commentary. Philadelphia, 1912.

HARRIS, R. The Voyage of Hanno. Cambridge, England, 1928.

BLÁZQUEZ, A. El Periplo de Himilco. Madrid, 1909.

Köster, H. Die Geographischen Kentnisse des Aischylus. Kiel, 1928.

Rawlinson, G. The History of Herodotus; an English version with copious notes and appendices. 4 vols. London, 1858–60.

Diels, H. Herodot und Hecataios. Hermes, 1887.

How, W. W., and Wells, J. A Commentary on Herodotus. 2 vols. Oxford, 1912.

Godley, A. D. Herodotus; with an English translation. 4 vols. Loeb Classical Library. London, 1920–24.

Brownson, C. L. Xenophon's Anabasis; with an English translation. Loeb Classical Library. London, 1922.

Strecker, W. Über den Rückzug der Zehntausend. Berlin, 1886.

von Hoffmeister, E. Durch Armenien, eine Wanderung und der Zug Xenophons bis zum Schwarzen Meere. Leipzig, 1911.

Fabricius, B. The Periplus of Scylax. Leipzig, 1878.

Bolchert, P. Aristoteles Erdkunde von Asien und Libyen. Berlin, 1908.

Robson, E. I. Arrian, Anabasis Alexandri, Books I–IV; with an English translation. Loeb Classical Library. London, 1929.

McCrindle, J. W. The Invasion of India by Alexander the Great, as described by Arrian, Q. Curtius, Diodorus, Plutarch, and Justin. Westminster, 1896.

McCrindle, J. W. Ancient India, as described by Megasthenes and Arrian; a translation of the fragments of the Indika of Megasthenes and the Indika of Arrian. London, 1926.

Stein, A. On Alexander's Track to the Indus. London, 1929.

Hergt, G. Pytheas. Halle, 1893.

Blázquez, A. Pyteas de Marsella. Madrid, 1913.

Seaton, R. C. The Argonautica of Apollonius Rhodius; with an English translation. Loeb Classical Library. London, 1912.

Berger, H. Die Geographischen Fragmente des Eratosthenes. Leipzig, 1880.

Thalamas, A. La Géographie d'Eratosthène. Paris, 1921.

Berger, H. Die Geographischen Fragmente des Hipparch. Leipzig, 1869.

Paton, W. R. The Histories of Polybius; with an English translation. 6 vols. Loeb Classical Library. London, 1922–27.

Stiehle, R. Der Geograph Artemidorus von Ephesus. Philologus, 1856.

EDWARDS, H. J. Caesar's Gallic War; with an English translation. Loeb Classical Library. London, 1922.

BECKMAN, F. Geographie und Ethnographie in Caesars Bellum
Gallicum. Dortmund, 1930.

HOLMES, T. R. Ancient Britain and the Invasions of Julius
Caesar. Oxford, 1907.

KLOTZ, A. Cäsarstudien, nebst einer Analyse der Strabonischen
Beschreibung von Gallien und Britannien. Leipzig, 1910.

VOGEL, F., and FISCHER, C. T. Diodori Bibliotheca Historica.
5 vols. Leipzig, 1888–1906.

ROLFE, J. C. Sallust; with an English translation. Loeb Classical
Library. London, 1920.

SCHOFF, W. H. Parthian Stations of Isidore of Charax. Philadelphia, 1914.

DETLEFSON, D. Ursprung, Einrichtung, und Bedeutung der
Erdkarte Agrippas. Berlin, 1906.

BUTZER, H. Über Strabos Geographica, insbesondere über Plan
und Ausführung des Werkes und Strabos Stellung zu seiner
Vorgängern. Frankfurt, 1887.

DUBOIS, M. Examen de la Géographie de Strabon. Paris, 1891.

HAMILTON, H. C., and FALCONER, W. The Geography of Strabo;
literally translated. 3 vols. Bohn's Classical Library. London, 1892–93.

TOZER, H. F. Selections from Strabo; with an introduction on
Strabo's life and works. Oxford, 1893.

MEINEKE, A. Strabonis Geographica. 3 vols. Leipzig, 1895–99.

KÄHLER, F. Strabos Bedeutung für die Moderne Geographie.
Halle, 1900.

FORBIGER, A. Strabos Erdbeschreibung übersetzt und durch
Anmerkungen erläutert. Stuttgart, 1905–08.

PAIS, E. Ancient Italy; translated from the Italian. Chicago,
1908. (For the date of Strabo's work.)

JONES, H. L. Strabo's Geography; with an English translation;
8 vols. (7 have appeared). Loeb Classical Library. London,
1917 ff.

PARTHEY, G. Pomponius Mela. Berlin, 1867.

FRICK, C. Pomponius Mela, De Chorographia. Leipzig, 1880.

MAYHOFF, C. Pliny's Natural History. Leipzig, 1906–08.

BOSTOCK, J., and RILEY, H. T. The Natural History of Pliny.
6 vols. Bohn's Classical Library. London, 1856–93.

DETLEFSON, D. Die Anordnung der Geographischen Bücher des Plinius und ihre Quellen. Berlin, 1909.

FURNEAUX, H. Cornelii Taciti Vita Agricolae. Oxford, 1898.

HUTTON, M. The Agricola and Germania of Tacitus; with an English translation. Loeb Classical Library. London, 1925.

FABRICIUS, B. Der Periplus des Erythraeischen Meeres. Leipzig, 1883.

SCHOFF, W. H. The Periplus of the Erythraean Sea; translated from the Greek and annotated. New York, 1912.

NOBBE, C. F. A. Ptolemy, Geographia. Leipzig, 1843–45.

MÜLLER, C., and FISCHER, C. T. Claudii Ptolemaei Geographia. 2 vols. Paris, 1883–1901.

RYLANDS, T. G. The Geography of Ptolemy Elucidated. Dublin, 1893.

GERINI, G. Ptolemy's Geography of Eastern Asia. London, 1909.

CUNTZ, O. Die Geographia des Ptolemaeus, Galliae, Germania, Raetia, Noricum, Pannoniae, Illyricum, Italia. Berlin, 1923.

RENOU, L. La Géographie de Ptolemée; l'Inde. Paris, 1925.

PARTHEY, G., and PINDER, M. Itinerarium Antonini Augusti et Hierosolymitanum. Berlin, 1848.

MILLER, K. Itineraria Romana. Stuttgart, 1916.

CUNTZ, O. Itineraria Romana; vol. I, Itineraria Antonini Augusti et Burdigalense. Leipzig, 1929.

MILLER, K. Die Weltkarte des Castorius genannt die Peutingersche Tafel. Ravensburg, 1887.

MILLER, K. Die Peutingersche Tafel oder Weltkarte des Castorius, mit kurzer Erklärung und Faksimile. Stuttgart, 1916.

MÜLLER, L. Claudius Rutilius Namatianus. Leipzig, 1870.

KEENE, C. H., and SAVAGE-ARMSTRONG, G. F. Rutilii Claudii Namatiani De Reditu suo Libri Duo. London, 1906.

MÜLLER, C. Geographi Graeci Minores. 2 vols. Paris, 1855–82.

RIESE, A. Geographi Latini Minores. Heilbroun, 1878.

MÜLLER, C. Fragmenta Historicorum Graecorum. 5 vols. Paris, 1878–85.

III

Miscellaneous Works on various aspects of the subject; listed in the Order of Publication

Movers, F. K. Die Phönizier. Bonn, 1841–56.

Vivien de Saint-Martin, L. Études de Géographie Ancienne et d'Ethnographie Asiatique. Paris, 1850–52.

Neumann, C. Die Hellenen im Skythenlande. Berlin, 1855.

Vivien de Saint-Martin, L. Étude sur la Géographie Grecque et Latine de l'Inde. Paris, 1858–60.

Vivien de Saint-Martin, L. Le Nord de l'Afrique dans l'Antiquité. Paris, 1863.

Smith, G. The Cassiterides. London, 1863.

Cunningham, A. The Ancient Geography of India. London, 1871.

McCrindle, J. W. The Commerce and Navigation of the Erythraean Sea. Calcutta, 1879.

Pietschmann, R. Geschichte der Phönizier. Berlin, 1889.

Rawlinson, G. The Story of Phoenicia. London, 1889.

McCrindle, J. W. Ancient India as Described in Classical Literature. Westminster, 1901.

Champault, P. Phéniciens et Grecs en Italie d'après l'Odyssée. Paris, 1906.

Baikie, J. The Sea-kings of Crete. London, 1910.

Mosso, A. The Dawn of Mediterranean Civilization; translated from the Italian. London, 1910.

Yule, H. Cathay and the Way Thither. 4 vols. London, 1913–16.

Dussaud, R. Les Civilisations Préhelleniques dans le Bassin de la Mer Égée. Paris, 1914.

Reese, W. Die Griechischen Nachrichten über Indien bis zum Feldzuge Alexanders des Grossen. Leipzig, 1914.

Mooney, W. W. Travel among the Ancient Romans. Boston, 1920.

Hermann, A. Die Verkehrswege zwischen China, India, und Rom um 100 nach Christen Geburt. Leipzig, 1922.

Fimmen, D. Die Kretisch-Mykenische Kultur. Leipzig, 1924.

Spence, L. The Problem of Atlantis. London, 1924.

Bacon, J. R. The Voyage of the Argonauts. London, 1925.

CHILDE, V. G. The Dawn of European Civilization. London,
    1925.
GLOTZ, G. The Aegean Civilization; translated from the French.
    London, 1925.
COUTENAU, G. La Civilisation Phénicienne. Paris, 1926.
CHARLESWORTH, M. P. Trade-routes and Commerce of the
    Roman Empire. Cambridge, England, 1926.
RAWLINSON, H. G. Intercourse between India and the Western
    World from the Earliest Times to the Fall of Rome. Cam-
    bridge, England, 1926.
WARMINGTON, E. H. The Commerce between the Roman Em-
    pire and India. Cambridge, England, 1928.

INDEX

INDEX